Sima's
Healthy Indulgence

Sima's Healthy Indulgence

100 Revamped, Guilt-Free Recipes to Transform Your Life

Sima Cohen
N.A.S.M. FNS

Photography by Delaram Pourabdi

Skyhorse Publishing

Contents

"The more you praise and celebrate your life, the more there is in life to celebrate."
—Oprah Winfrey

Acknowledgments

Have you heard the cliché "it takes a village"? Well, it's true. I wouldn't be able to do what I do, nor would I have been able to produce this incredible book without *my* village. However, before talking about my village, let me mention a couple important people in my life.

First is Kayla Sorensen, my beautiful daughter. You are the love of my life, my princess love, and a true gift from God. I am privileged to be your mother. You are the biggest blessing in my life. I know I am here to guide you as your mom, but in so many ways I feel that you teach me what's really important in life.

Then, I would like to thank my partner, the savvy Farhad David Rostamian, whose dedication, insight, and incredible eye for detail—not to mention his love for cooking and food—has helped us make something above my expectations. David, in a way, I feel that you and I have co-created this book together, as your vision and leadership have been captured throughout the pages and have taken this project to a whole new level.

Speaking of my village, let me introduce this incredible team. Minoti Vaishnav, my gratitude for capturing the essence of my work into words, I appreciate and thank you for your unique gift. Our prop and food stylist, Leslie Rodriguez, your dedication to your craft and your no-nonsense attitude makes you an integral part of our team. Delaram Pourabdi, our amazing photographer, your artistic vision and photography skills have brought this book to life. It is a breath of fresh air to see how your photos captured the essence of my recipes and showcased them as the mouth-watering dishes they are. Madeline Hodges, our set designer, your creative approach to styling and designing dishes for photography was instrumental in transforming our vision on the set. Justin Hall, our skilled videographer, thank you for capturing so vividly all that happened behind the scene as we made this book. Melissa Duenas, I appreciate your detailed work on this project as it allowed me to focus on what I do best in writing this book. Lastly, Kristine Lacayanga, thank you for assisting me throughout this project, from proofreading to preparing the final manuscript. Your attention to details and organizational adherence supported this project above and behind.

I am also extremely grateful to collaborate with several world-renowned brands and professionals, including the extraordinary people that supported the creation of this cookbook. Robert Schuller and Nick Quintero from Melissa's Produce (you guys rock), Sadaf foods, Alkaline heals you, Wellness to be, Justin's, Gomacro, Primal Kitchen, Panorama meats, Eden foods, reCAP mason jars, Fitvine wine, Harmless harvest, Frontier co-op, Clover juice, Philosophie, The Berry man, Purely Elizabeth, Sari foods, Suja juice—thank you all for believing in me and my work.

Throughout my journey that led to the creation of this book, I have had the privilege of meeting and studying under the guidance of world-class mentors. The most impactful among them is *New York Times* bestselling author Marianne Williamson. She has been the greatest influence in my growth both personally and professionally as her teachings have led me through my own life transformation. Marianne, I thank you for your brilliance, wisdom, and guidance. I am beyond grateful to call you my mentor and friend.

Abigail Gehring and Leah Zarra and the entire Skyhorse Publishing team, I am grateful for your patience and grace as you steered this project from the outset, and worked with me to bring this book to the world. I am very happy to have had the privilege of having my first book published by Skyhorse and their elite team.

I have had the good fortune of working with many talented professionals throughout my career. Clyde Haygood, Shira Wintner, and Cynthia Salazar: I am indebted to your hard work and believing in me and my crazy dreams. To my good friends, Shirin Yadegar, founder of *LA Mom* magazine, and Shahriar and Atoosa Rad, this project would not have been possible without your kindness and generosity. You opened your doors and graciously let us wash, prep, chop, cook, blend, mix, spice, bake, burn, stage, design, photograph, record, and otherwise mess up your beautiful homes—and let us do it over and over again. We are forever grateful.

I was born into an incredible and loving family, one that taught me about the important blessings in life such as culture, food, community, *Shabbat* celebrations, and having strong roots and bonds, and for that I am truly grateful. To my mother (Tamar), brothers (Itzik, David, Avi), and sisters (Galit and Limor), I may not see you as often as I would like, but I want you to know that you have given me so much meaning and unconditional love as we grew up together. And to my dad (Israel) and my loving grandparents who are watching over me from above: I love you, and I know you are proud of me.

I truly have the *best* clients in the world to whom I would like to pay a special tribute. For starters, I wish I could mention each and every one of you. You have been with me for the past twenty years, and I cannot express enough how proud I am of all of you. When you look at me and tell me "You've changed my life," I know why I do what I do. Your transformation continues to be my greatest reward.

Without my hardships, struggles, breakdowns, and hard lessons, I would not be the person that I am today. All of those hard moments and difficult experiences in my life turned out to be blessings; they have resulted in breakthroughs, and I am grateful for having lived and learned through them all. Also, I want to personally extend my gratitude and appreciation to one incredible woman who inspired me to live my life in a way that I learned people around me are the ones who matter the most. Even though she isn't physically near me, she is someone that exuded such influence in my life which made me want to better my life and help better the lives of others. I idolize the life that she created for herself and for so many millions of others around the world. Oprah Winfrey, I want to thank you from the bottom of my heart for being who you are and what you do for others, I commend you and look up to you. So at the end, let me acknowledge all women out there, especially single moms who may have gone through or are currently experiencing the same hardships. I may not know you personally, but I walk in your shoes every day and encourage you to embrace each and every struggle with your inner strength and strong will. We share many common goals and strive to have balance in our lives. You are the backbone of your family and I salute you, your hard work and dedication. Wherever you are, I want you to know that I am wholeheartedly rooting for you as my soul sisters.

Introduction

Hi. I'm Sima, and I would like to welcome you to my world of Healthy Indulgence. I know what you're thinking—*how can Sima's cookbook help me with my health and nutrition goals, especially with weight loss, yet still allow me to indulge?* Well, as we discover in the healthy indulgences throughout this book, I promise you will enjoy the journey as much as the destination. But before we start indulging, you need to know who I am and what led me to create this cookbook.

I was born in a small town near Tel Aviv, into a large family where I was the oldest of six children, living with my parents in a tiny two-bedroom apartment. I grew up in a rough neighborhood, an environment that toughened me up from a very early age and helped me withstand many of my future challenges. During my childhood, food was in abundance, but our lifestyle was very simple with no luxuries and access to only basic necessities. While we lacked variety and luxury, our lives were enriched with rituals and traditions. We had great respect for food, and eating together as a family was the norm. Food was not to be wasted (God forbid!), or disregarded in any shape or form; food was a big part of my childhood. With that upbringing, at the age of eleven, I decided to move to a Kibbutz (a farming and co-op community that is still common in Israel) in search of a better education and life. At eighteen years old, like all other young adults in the country, I joined the military for mandatory service. While I didn't serve in a war, my military experience taught me necessary discipline for physical training and endurance—qualities that shaped a big part of my future. When I turned twenty, I decided to follow my intuition and my longtime dream, and moved to the US, settling in Los Angeles.

As Los Angeles became my new home, I found myself attracted to the powerful vibe of the city, and its fixation on physical attraction. Every billboard, every advertisement, every TV show, every music video, every live performance, and every movie showcased a fascination with perfect bodies and physical form. Crazy diets, extreme plastic surgeries, and intense exercise programs were the norm. At the time, I was young, naïve, and very impressionable in my new la la land, and got caught up in the craze. Obsessed with body image and trying to fit in in this new city, I tried starvation diets and extreme exercise programs. Slowly, food went from being a blessing to being a curse; eating became a forbidden and guilty activity. Being good was synonymous with eating nothing, and eating anything was synonymous with feeling guilty—a complete switch from my experience with food growing up. At that time, I had already professionally started coaching clients on weight loss and nutrition, yet I was very stressed out about my own yo-yo dieting and excessive exercise routines. While I have never been obese or overweight, I still struggled with my diet and body image. This made me feel like I'd lost control, until Thanksgiving 2001, when I found out I was pregnant with my daughter.

Frustrated with my inability to control my food intake, I had to immediately stop dieting and counting calories, stop measuring quantities and obsessing over why I couldn't have a particular food. Once I stopped my obsessing about food, I was able to recognize the destructive cycle I was in. I discovered that everything started with my thoughts. My thoughts became the foundation of my world; they drove my actions and decisions, including food choices that fed my body. My mind was the cause and my body was the effect. I had discovered that the more I told myself I couldn't have something, the more I craved it. As you might guess, bread and chocolate topped my list of "bad" foods.

My breakthrough started when I realized the only way to change my "body" (and my body image) was to change my "mind" and my thinking. I knew very well all the disciplines related to sweat (exercise) and substance (food), but it was only when I incorporated the third element (self) that my foundation for healthy living was finally strong. I thoroughly experienced why food alone (or food and exercise together) is not the complete answer. I figured out that nothing could permanently change in my body unless and until I awakened the "self" and nurtured it to take charge of my life, my sustenance, and all the decisions that ultimately influence what I eat.

Instead of constantly forcing myself to avoid carbs all together, I started to incorporate complex carbohydrates into my meals (except at nights; you will read more about principles of my PCF combo diet later). The addition of small amount of low glycemic complex carbohydrates had the biological effect of stabilizing my blood sugar and eliminating insulin spikes, a scientifically proven factor that can heavily influence how our bodies naturally regulate weight and burning calories with ease, rather than storing them.

With that breakthrough, as my "self" started to regain control, after years of hard work and absolute adherence to my three "S" elements (self, sweat, substance), amazing things started to happen in my life. All my obsessions with weight and body image slowly melted away and were replaced with a healthy image of my "self." All my cravings for bread and chocolate, all my lethargic low energy days, all my guilty feelings about food finally said their farewell. Self-doubt was replaced with self-confidence and self-love. Food, once again, became a blessing in my life as my mind was able to see it as sustenance, not just calories; I felt the joy of fueling my body as opposed to feeling guilty after eating. My search to find a method for a healthy life was complete, as I had found the answer for me in the interplay between self, sweat, and substance. This book is dedicated to enjoying the best "substance"—the type that promotes weight loss yet is also satisfying. It's the true experience of healthy indulging.

This personal transformation also drove my professional work as a personal trainer, nutritionist, and life coach. For over two decades I have been working one-on-one with countless clients from all walks of life, men and women, young teens and seniors, business moguls, celebrities, single moms, teachers, starving artists, and everything in between. Whether we come from a ritzy Manhattan high-rise or a hidden small farm in Montana, the common thread among us all is that we are on a journey to optimal health, but don't want guilt and self-doubt to accompany us. And that is precisely my experience and the foundation of my method and recipes hand-picked in this book. *Sima's Healthy Indulgence* is not about deprivation or counting calories; rather it's about a life of abundance and embracing all the blessings that come with food.

There are arbitrary turns in life and a different turn would have taken you to another place, another cookbook, and another author. Yet, you are here with me. Unexpectedly good things can happen, when you decide to take charge of your life. Unthinkably good things will happen when you open your heart and look at food not as what controls you, rather as the wondrous substance that it is. Unpredictably good things will happen when you eat and live guilt-free; experiencing food in abundance and losing weight. Unimaginably good things are waiting for you when you embrace what I have prepared here—100 healthy indulgences ready in 30 minutes or less.

Indulge!

With love and gratitude,

Sima

Seven Things You Probably Don't Know About Me

In my twenty years of experience with working with my clients, I shared a lot of history and aspects of my personal life, while I kept a few things close to my heart. Now, I am going to reveal a few of those secrets to you to help you get to know me a little better.

1. I'm superstitious.
You won't catch me walking under ladders or crossing my legs when I sit in meetings. I'm a big believer in energy, and anything that comes with a negative connotation raises my radar. When I want things to go well, I often knock on wood.

2. I love bread. It's one of my guilty pleasures.
Crunchy, nutty, grainy—I love all types of bread. But I have also disciplined myself to limit to one slice. Yes, I do practice what I preach, most of the time!

3. I loathe injections and needles.
I am a very fearless woman. However, I cannot even begin to describe how fearful I am of needles. It's like I am ready to pass out the moment the nurse approaches me for even a simple vaccine injection. In fact, thinking about it now is raising my heart rate.

4. I do strength training, run, hike, and practice hot yoga.
Working out and exercising is a part of my DNA. It's a part of my life. It hasn't always been like this for me and I admit there are times that I don't enjoy it. However, I am well-disciplined, and have accepted that exercise is an important part of life—just like working, or being a parent. It has become second nature to me.

5. I am extremely intuitive.
Have you ever had a moment where you're thinking about someone and you see his or her name written on a magazine or billboard? Or your phone rings and you know who

is calling you before you even look at the name on your caller ID? That happens to me all the time. I let my intuition guide me, and I've almost always been right.

6. I have never eaten sushi.
And I am not planning on ever trying it; it's just not going to happen.

7. My daughter is the love of my life. Times a billion.
There aren't enough words in the English dictionary to describe how crazy I am about my daughter. I strive to make the world a better place for her and all children everywhere, and work hard to make sure she lives a happy life full of abundance and gratitude.

The Healthy Indulgence Philosophy

What exactly is the Healthy Indulgence plan all about? Simply put, it's about living with abundance, with appreciation, and with gratitude for all we have. It's about indulging without guilt, and by counting our blessings and not by counting calories or by deprivation.

Here is how you begin your new relationship with food based on the Healthy Indulgence philosophy:

1. Quitting the vicious cycle of suffering and dieting.
The first thing you have to comprehend is that excessive dieting is not going to solve your weight-loss or nutrition dilemmas. Quitting food is not the answer. Quitting your diet is.

2. Resolving to do better.
It's one thing to say you're quitting your diet. It's another thing to *actually* quit your diet. Once you make the choice to curb unhealthy eating habits, stick to your decision and put that resolution into practice. As I always say: *knowing* is one thing, but *doing* is completely another.

3. Understanding that the decisions that you make now affect the rest of your life.
Are you indecisive? Have you put off making up your mind about something because you don't want to face the effort that comes with making that decision? The truth is, being indecisive or passive is a decision too, because you're deciding not to take action. You must recognize that every decision you make—or refuse to make—influences the rest of your life. Be wise and ask yourself what you really need to do. Then do it.

4. Understanding that losing weight is just the cherry on top of this way of life.
The Healthy Indulgence plan is not a weight-loss program; it's a healthy living plan. Weight-loss is an effect of this program, but it is not the sole goal of this program. Changing your lifestyle will bring weight loss with it, but you must focus on the overall strategy of this plan to truly benefit from it.

5. Understanding that this is all on *your* terms.

It's not on my terms or anyone else's terms. This plan is all about *you*, your needs, and your goals. There's no sugarcoating nor are there any empty promises in this plan. I'm here to be your GPS and guide you on your journey to a healthier life. Just remember every decision you make, what you eat, and how you feel is under your control.

The Healthy Indulgence Plan

Everything that I have created has always been about my clients' specific needs and requirements. Before I started crafting the Healthy Indulgence plan, my clients would tell me that they had a sweet tooth, or that they were hungry for "forbidden" food and wanted to eat it without guilt. Some had no energy, and some were overweight. Some had severe medical conditions and limitations. And yet some just wanted to lose the last stubborn ten pounds. Hearing these declarations instantly made something click inside of me, and I knew it was time to create nutrition plans and indulgent recipes that would help them overcome food guilt, lose weight, attain healthier, leaner, stronger bodies, and experience a happier, more fulfilled life.

The first step to your healthy living is to fully understand what that means. Healthy living means being able to have a healthy love affair with food—being able to celebrate a guiltless freedom that excludes deprivation, counting calories, or measuring body fat. It is that primal instinct that blossoms from within you—instincts to live, laugh, and love, and be the best version of yourself. It's about extending that philosophy to your body, and living a life that radiates authenticity, happiness, and purpose without depriving or compromising yourself. When you approach every day with a positive attitude and determination to take care of yourself, you will realize that how you think, what you eat, and the way you feel, will elevate your life to a whole new level. Then, losing weight is just the cherry on top of your delicious, indulgent living.

Incorporating Healthy Indulgences into Your Lifestyle

In order to begin the Healthy Indulgence plan, the first thing I would like you to do is look within yourself and stop self-sabotaging behaviors. I know you have heard it a thousand times, but let's make this the last time. Stop disrespecting yourself or obsessing about mistakes you have made or regrets about the past. Examine any fears of failure you may have, and discontinue behaviors that make you drive yourself to madness by putting your body under a strict diet. There is no quick fix to changing your life forever or correcting months and years of yo-yo dieting. It takes dedication, time, and hard work, as well as tools and methods. However, together we can build a strong foundation that will support you on your journey to a better life.

Once you've decided you're done with self-sabotage, start feeding your mind and body with the blueprints outlined in this book. For example, one of these guidelines is to add meditation or another type of spiritual practice to your daily routine. Be it prayer or deep breathing exercises, journaling, or creating vision boards, whatever your preference, we all need to mentally check in with ourselves from time to time. So make sure you check in with yourself regularly. As for your body, you need to stop seeing food as the enemy and instead start seeing it as a source of energy and sustenance. Your sustenance is the source of your being and what sustains you. Feed your mind and body well.

Meditation and self-care are broad ideas, and while those are important, I want to give you some specific tools that you can incorporate into your routine and lifestyle. With that, I give you:

Top 10 Techniques to Help You Get into the Best Shape of Your Life

1. Do cardio first thing in the morning before breakfast, and last thing at night after dinner to maximize your fat burning capabilities.
2. Wear a sweat belt while doing cardio—sweat belts help shrink your waistline and tighten your core.
3. Use a sauna or steam room 2–3 times per week to release toxins.
4. Follow my Healthy Indulgence PCF combo plan to help stabilize your blood sugar and keep cravings at bay. Do not skip meals or snacks.
5. H_2O. Water! Water! Water! I can't emphasize this enough. Not only does water curb hunger, but it also keeps you hydrated and regulates your bowel movements.
6. Coffee? Yes. Okay. But only if you drink it black with no cream or sugar.
7. Superfoods are a great addition to your diet because they are packed with an ample amount of nutrients. Your entire diet doesn't have to be chock full of superfoods; even a small amount will make a big difference.
8. Meditate: Take care of your psyche and embed into your subconscious that your health is your wealth. Getting in the best shape of your life and losing weight isn't just about making sure the number on the scale is less than the month before. It's a lifelong commitment that takes energy and practice to maintain.

9. Have yams (or sweet potatoes), eggs, and cooked chicken in your fridge, ready to go.

10. Weight training is essential to your workout regime. There is a plethora of benefits, one of which includes increasing your stamina so you can work stronger and longer. Another benefit of weight training? It increases the strength of tissues, muscles, and tendons. Weight training is just as important as cardio, so get those weights working!

Follow the Healthy Indulgence Philosophy and incorporate my techniques into your lifestyle, and you will not only see weight-loss results, but you will also find that you have more energy, increased stamina, and a stronger immune system.

Self, Sweat, Substance

Following the Healthy Indulgence plan is easy. There are three main elements to keep in mind.

Element #1: Self

If I asked you to describe yourself, what would you say? You might choose to list your physical characteristics, like tall, short, skinny, curvy, brunette, blonde, or other adjectives used to describe appearance. Conversely, you might choose to describe your personality with words like genuine, positive, adventurous, ambitious, loyal, driven, or any other words you feel describe who you are at your core.

While the words I listed above are all positive, some people choose to describe themselves with negative language. Insecure, unsuccessful, meek, unhappy . . . the list goes on. If you've got harmful words on your list, it's time to start addressing why you feel this way about yourself.

The road to better health starts from within you, and the way you see and feel about yourself is a crucial component to achieving your nutrition goals. It's important to look within yourself and figure out what makes you see yourself in a certain light. If you discover that you've been self-sabotaging, this is the first problem you must fix. You have the power to change your life, but harnessing this power is the key to propelling forward.

Having ownership over your thoughts, feelings, and actions will help you change destructive patterns and behaviors that cause you to make bad food decisions. Additionally, if you do have a lapse in judgment, I want you to understand that it's okay to give yourself a break. We're all human. The harsher you are with yourself, the worse it is for your overall physical and mental well-being. So forgive yourself. Love yourself, and the rest will follow.

Element #2: Sweat

I get it. Most people aren't crazy about working out. We don't like to sweat because it makes us feel sticky and uncomfortable. The effort of working out also comes with muscle pain and breathlessness. While I agree that working out isn't the most comfortable activity at first, it is an important element to being healthy and losing weight.

I often hear that people don't have time to work out because of their busy, hectic schedules. I understand. However, *everyone* has a busy, hectic schedule and yet people still manage to make time for the things that are important to them.

If you make exercising a priority, you will find that not only does the workout get easier, but you also start enjoying it and looking forward to it more and more. Working out doesn't have to take over your life and you don't have to spend three hours a day in a gym to achieve the results you want. The Healthy Indulgence specialized workout routine can be done anywhere and it takes less time than you think. The workout only requires two dumbbells and a yoga mat, and is individually targeted to your needs.

There's something else to keep in mind about working out. If you aspire to lose weight and live a healthier lifestyle, you cannot escape working out. If you're looking for a shortcut, sorry, but there isn't one. Somewhere deep inside of you, you know you need to exercise to achieve the lifestyle and body you desire.

Element #3: Substance

Substance means fuel, energy, and life. The right fuel to give you the energy you need to live a long, healthy, and satisfying life. Think of it as eating more wholesome, quality food that does not come from a factory, does not contain anything artificial, and is free from any additives or chemicals.

Dieting Explained

What is a diet? It's a program that tells you to stop consuming certain types of food. Diets can be dangerous because not only do they keep you from ingesting all the nutrients you need, but they also affect the way you perceive food. You've probably heard of diets that will tell you what to do, but they won't explain how these actions can help you and your body in the long run. This is why most diets are short-lived and do not work for everyone. In short, their usefulness and longevity is limited.

Sima's Healthy Indulgence will teach you about specific food combinations that will allow you to eat more frequently, stabilize your blood sugar, speed up your metabolism, regulate hormones, and burn fat faster. As stated before, the Healthy Indulgence plan is not a diet. It is a way of life that works to improve your mind, body, and soul. We believe in focusing on the whole rather than just on specific parts, and when you follow the principles outlined in the book, you will maximize your full potential.

As you continue to read *Sima's Healthy Indulgence*, you will learn how to have a better relationship with food by combining foods in correct combination that I call

PCF: power proteins, complex carbs, and friendly fats. Follow my PCF combination for every meal (except dinner, when you substitute carbs for vegetables) and you will stabilize your blood sugar, activate your body's natural fat burning power, and be on the road to the healthiest you've ever been. This powerful and proven method for eating is described further in the next section.

PCF Combination: The Pillars of the Healthy Indulgence Plan

Are you staring at the title of this chapter and wondering how carbs and fats can possibly help you? You're probably used to hearing the word "protein" thrown around when it comes to healthy eating, but are carbs and fats really key components to helping you achieve your nutritional goals?

Absolutely. Yes. Without a doubt. Knowing what to eat, what time to eat it, and what foods to combine with each other, is the optimal way to get your body into top shape.

Don't worry. You'll understand just what I mean in a few moments. When you combine power protein, complex carbs, and friendly fats with each other and consume them at certain times of the day, you experience the safest, fastest, and most sustainable weight loss possible. In the next few paragraphs you will learn how to combine foods in correct combinations, and how doing this can not only help you lose weight, but also stabilize your blood sugar and activate your body's natural fat-burning power. So, let's take a look at how PCF works.

Protein, carbs, and fats are three micronutrients that are found in all food sources. For our bodies to function properly, we need all three. Sadly, many diets restrict or completely eliminate consumption of one or more of the three micronutrients. Such an approach to diet not only starves our bodies and brains from receiving necessary nourishment, it also robs us from our natural ability to regulate and maintain ideal body weight. So instead, I recommend and promote a diet based on all of the three elements.

The PCF food plan has even more benefits than just regulating your metabolism and your blood sugar—this combination also helps balance your hormones. A large percentage of the population of the United States has a problem with obesity, and what most people don't know is that this obesity isn't just caused by overeating. It's also caused by poor diet choices such as processed food and junk food. These types of food not only promote weight gain, they also contribute to hormonal imbalances. When your hormones are out of whack, your body is unable to function efficiently. The hormonal imbalance in turn causes cravings and binging, contributing to weight gain.

This is where a PCF diet comes in. Proteins and carbs get along famously, bringing together their unique properties in a perfect harmony.

Not only is protein vital to the satisfaction of our bodies after we eat, but protein is also required for the restoration and building of our body's cells, tissues, and organs. According to a study in the *American Journal of Clinical Nutrition*[1], "protein is more effective at satisfying hunger than either carbohydrates or fat." So, by having protein with every meal, your body will get to a point where it is completely satisfied until your next meal.

Carbs are necessary for your body in a different but equally crucial way. Carbs can be broken down into simple carbs and complex carbs. Simple carbs can provide your body with quick bursts of energy (think orange juice) while complex carbs will provide your body with long-lasting energy (think yam or sweet potato).

While Protein and Carbs are good for you, let's not forget about Friendly Fats. The reason for eating fats with your food can be explained by going back to the topic of hormones. To understand why fat is important, let's look at leptin, one of the hormones that shapes our appetite and hunger.

The function of leptin is to communicate to our brain how much fat we're carrying and whether or not we are hungry. Typically, if our blood leptin levels are low, our bodies keep signaling to our brains that we are hungry. Leptin levels rise as we eat so that our bodies know when we'd had enough to eat. However, if a person is overweight or obese, their hormones may not be functioning properly, which means they may be resistant to the effects of leptin. This means that when they're eating, they won't know when to stop because their leptin levels will not be able to communicate satiety or fullness to their brain.

Enter Friendly Fats! Leptin is produced in your fat cells, so if you take out the fat, your body will hold on to every last pound in fear that soon all the fat will be gone. So what should you do? Give your body the fat it wants, but make sure this fat comes from good sources like fish, coconut, coconut oil, avocados, extra-virgin olive oil, and nuts, instead of deep fried food such as french fries.

By combining carbs, proteins, and fats, you will fuel your body optimally, achieve your weight loss goals, and keep up an energy level that sustains you for long periods

---

1   Russell J de Souza, Janis F Swain, Lawrence J Appel, and Frank M Sacks. Alternatives for macronutrient intake and chronic disease: a comparison of the OmniHeart diets with popular diets and with dietary recommendations, Am J Clin Nutr July 2008 88: 1–11.

of time. *Sima's Healthy Indulgence* plan gives you a plethora of recipe ideas on what to eat for your PCF combination. A healthy PCF combination throughout the day will also help you avoid food cravings, and choose healthier food options.

Here are a few rules of thumb for consuming Proteins, Carbs, and Fats:

- Proteins: 4–6 ounces per meal (think of it as about the size of the palm of your hand) and about 2 ounces per snack.
- Carbs: ½–¾ cup cooked carbs per meal (equivalent to the fist of your hand) and about ¼ cup per snack.
- Fats: 1–2 tablespoons (or equivalent to the length of your thumb) and about ½ a tablespoon per snack.

To help you understand exactly which foods fall under which pillar, here's a handy chart you can refer to in order to determine what to eat:

POWER PROTEINS

- Meat
  - Flank steak
  - Skirt steak
  - Filet mignon
  - 80% ground lean beef, preferably grass-fed and organic
  - Deli meat, nitrate free
- Poultry
  - Chicken breast, boneless and skinless
  - Eggs
  - Turkey breast
  - Turkey sausage, nitrate free
  - Turkey bacon
- Seafood
  - Shrimp
  - Oysters
  - Mussels
  - Fish
    - Albacore
    - Wild salmon
    - Sea bass
    - Black cod
    - Ahi tuna
    - Mahi mahi
    - Lox
    - Canned tuna, in water or olive oil
- Plant Based
  - Chia seeds
  - Edamame
  - Tofu
  - Tempeh
- Legumes
  - Beans
  - Lentils
  - Chickpeas
- Low-lactose Dairy
  - Greek yogurt
  - Feta cheese
  - Swiss cheese

COMPLEX CARBS

- Oats
  - Old-fashioned
  - Steel cut
- 100% Whole Wheat . . .
  - bread
  - pita bread
  - tortillas
  - Ezekiel bread
  - naan bread
- Amaranth
- Rice
  - Brown rice
  - Wild rice
- Quinoa/quinoa flakes
- Barley
- Selba crackers
- Cream of Wheat
- Farro
- Millet
- Sprouted grains
- Potatoes
- Sweet potatoes
- Yams
- Whole wheat couscous
- Muesli
- Buckwheat

FRIENDLY FATS

- Oils
  - Extra-virgin unrefined cold pressed coconut oil
  - Cold pressed olive oil
  - Flax oil
  - Grapeseed oil
  - Safflower oil
  - Sesame oil
  - Hemp oil
  - Udo's Oil
- Raw and Unsalted Nuts
  - Almonds
  - Brazil nuts
  - Cashews
  - Peanuts
  - Walnuts
- Hazelnuts
- Marcona almonds
- Pistachios
- Seeds
  - Chia seeds
  - Pumpkin seeds
  - Black and white sesame seeds
- Raw, Unsalted Nut Butters
  - Peanut
  - Almond
  - Cashew
  - Hazelnut
  - Macadamia
  - Avocado
- Green and black olives
- Unsweetened shredded coconut

Superfoods: The Superheroes of Food

Superfoods are all the rage in diet culture today, and though you may have heard about them only recently, superfoods have actually been around for centuries. Our ancestors used superfoods in their meals for several generations. They may not have coined the term "superfood," but they certainly used these ingredients for creating nutritious food and facilitating a healthy lifestyle.

Superfoods are nutrient-rich foods that are especially beneficial for health and well-being. However, this does not mean those are all we should eat; superfoods are meant to complement your diet, not completely take it over. We should use superfoods as an addition to the food we already eat because they elevate our diet, but we still need the right combination of proteins, carbs, and fats to stay healthy.

I have personally handpicked all the superfoods listed below. They are all loaded with vitamins, minerals, fiber, iron, and antioxidants, and have anti-inflammatory properties. Not only are they good for your health and help your body, immune system, and metabolism to function at the highest level, they're also wholesome, pure, flavorful, and delicious. Superfoods are unprocessed—they were not created in a lab. They are easy to incorporate into your meals and add flavor to your food. Each recipe in this book has an "Optional Superfood" column that gives you three different superfood options to add extra nutrients to your meal.

What counts as a superfood? On the next few pages, you will find a handy list to guide you.

SUPERFOOD	ORIGIN	PROPERTIES	HEALTH BENEFITS
Bee Pollen	Bee pollen is a pollen ball that has been packed by worker honeybees into pellets.	One of nature's most nourishing foods, bee pollen is high in protein and vitamins and is a good source of energy.	Clears up your skin, regulates your intestines, and aids recovery from chronic illness.
Black Garlic	Black garlic is basically caramelized garlic and it is often used in Asian cuisine.	Rich in amino acids. Also has almost double the amount of antioxidants in regular garlic.	Reduces inflammation, boosts immune function, is toxic to 14 types of cancer, and boosts cardiovascular health.
Unsweetened Cacao (powder and nibs)	Cacao is a dried and fully fermented seed that comes from tropical evergreen trees.	Rich in natural antioxidant compounds.	Cacao lowers the risk of heart disease and stabilizes your metabolism.
Chia Seeds	Chia seeds come from a species of flowering plant in the mint family. These plants are native to central and southern Mexico and Guatemala.	Contains healthy omega-3 fatty acids, carbohydrates, protein, fiber, antioxidants, and calcium.	Chia seeds help control your hunger and enhance your diet with super nutrients.
Flaxseeds	Comes from flax, a fiber crop that is cultivated all over the world, from China to Switzerland.	Flaxseeds contain good fats like omega-3 fatty acids.	Fights heart disease, cancer, and diabetes.
Goji Berries	Goji berries come from boxthorn plants that are native to the Asian continent.	Contain vitamin C, fiber, iron, vitamin A, zinc, and antioxidants.	Goji berries reduce the risk of diabetes, high blood pressure, and even optometric issues.
Hemp Seeds	Hemp seeds come from hemp plants typically found in the Northern Hemisphere.	A natural source of non-meat based protein.	Hemp seeds aid weight loss, increase energy levels, lower high blood pressure, and allow rapid recovery from disease and injury.
Wheat Germ	Wheat germ is a concentrated form of a wheat kernel.	A source of several essential nutrients like folic acid, vitamin E, zinc, magnesium, and essential fatty acids.	Boosts immunity and fights heart disease.

SUPERFOOD	ORIGIN	PROPERTIES	HEALTH BENEFITS
Acai	Acai is an indigenous berry commonly found in the rain forests of the Amazon.	Rich in antioxidants and vitamin C.	Lowers cholesterol levels in the blood stream, prevents blood clots, helps digestion, and aids in skin problems.
Coconut	Coconuts come from coconut palm trees and are more of a fruit than a nut.	The coconut is high in dietary fiber and contains a low glycemic index.	Coconut in all forms helps prevent obesity, reduces sweet cravings, improves digestion, and boosts energy.
Dates	Dates come from date palms, a flowering plant species in the palm tree family.	Rich in potassium, fiber, and magnesium.	Dates are proven to relieve constipation, heart problems, diarrhea, and intestinal disorders.
Lúcuma	Lúcuma is a fruit native to the Andean valleys and produced in Chile, Peru, and Ecuador.	Good source of antioxidants, dietary fiber, and vitamins including beta-carotene and niacin. It is also rich in minerals including zinc, potassium, calcium, magnesium, and iron.	Optimizes bodily functions and strengthens the immune system.
Pomegranate	Pomegranates grow on shrubs. They are typically in season in the Northern Hemisphere between September and February, and in the Southern Hemisphere from March to May.	Contains antioxidants, vitamin C, and vitamin K.	Lowers blood pressure and decreases the risk of heart disease.
Raw Tahini	Made from ground sesame seeds, tahini is used in a variety of middle-eastern cuisine.	An excellent source of calcium, manganese, amino acids, omega-3 and omega-6 fatty acids.	Promotes healthy cell growth, and prevents anemia.
Wheatgrass	Wheatgrass is prepared from the cotyledons of the common wheat plant and is found all over the world.	Contains vitamins A, B-complex, C, E, and K.	Increases red blood-cell count, and increases metabolism.

SUPERFOOD	ORIGIN	PROPERTIES	HEALTH BENEFITS
Amaranth	Amaranth grain comes from the amaranth plant. It has been cultivated as a grain for over 8,000 years and was once a staple of the Aztec diet.	A good source of protein, dietary fiber, and is rich in manganese, magnesium, iron, and selenium.	Lowers the risk of inflammation, diabetes, heart disease, and stroke.
Green Tea	Green tea is made from leaves that have not undergone the oxidation process like black tea. It originated in China but soon spread all over Asia.	Is anti-inflammatory and antibacterial.	Prevents cardiovascular disease and decreases cholesterol levels.
Harissa	Harissa is an African hot chili pepper paste made from roasted red peppers, spices, and herbs.	Is anti-inflammatory and antibacterial.	Lowers blood pressure and decreases the risk of heart disease and cancer.
Pumpkin Seeds	Pumpkin seeds are the edible seeds of a pumpkin. The seeds are usually flat and asymmetrical, and are light green in color.	High in zinc, vitamin K, vitamin B_6, and vitamin E. It is also anti-inflammatory.	Fights depression, lowers cholesterol, promotes good kidney health, and heals arthritis.

Spices

Spices deserve their own special section under the superfoods banner because they intensify flavors and add nutrients to your meal. On the next page, you'll find a few of my favorite spices:

NAME	ORIGIN	PROPERTIES	HEALTH BENEFITS
Black Pepper	Black pepper comes from a flowering vine plant. The plant is then cultivated for its fruit, and when dried, becomes the spice black pepper.	Rich source of manganese, iron, vitamin C, vitamin K, and dietary fiber.	Black pepper helps with respiratory disorders, indigestion, anemia, dental disease, and heart disease.
Cayenne Pepper	Cayenne comes from the capsicum (bell pepper) family, and can be grown in a variety of locations including tropical and temperate zones.	Rich in vitamin A, vitamin B, vitamin E, vitamin C, potassium, and manganese.	Increases blood flow and decreases the risk of heart disease and cancer.
Cinnamon	Cinnamon is a spice obtained from the inner bark of several different tree species.	Cinnamon is an antioxidant, is anti-inflammatory, and anti-microbial.	Boosts immunity, and protects against cancer and heart disease.
Maca	Maca comes from a plant native to the Andes Mountains of Peru.	Acts like an herb and has painkilling properties.	Helps with symptoms of menopause, PMS, and depression.
Sea Salt	Produced from the natural evaporation of seawater, rather than by being manually extracted from sedimentary deposits.	Rich in trace minerals, contains magnesium, calcium, and potassium.	Improves brain function, regulates muscle growth, and helps with digestive issues.
Turmeric Root	Turmeric is part of the ginger family. It grows in South Asia, and needs a considerable amount of rainfall to thrive.	Turmeric is anti-inflammatory, antifungal, and antibacterial.	Boosts immunity and protects against cancer and diabetes. Is also used for arthritis patients.

Natural Sweeteners

How much sugar have you consumed in your lifetime and why do you now get cravings for it? Do you have the willpower to turn down a piece of pie if it's in front of you? Are you using artificial sweeteners?

Your sweet tooth can be cured. But in order to get there, you have to understand the science behind why you crave sugar, and why sugar consumption is bad for your body.

Sugar: Bad.

What happens to our bodies when we eat sugar? A recent UC San Francisco study found that drinking soda ages your body on a cellular level at the same rate that cigarettes do[2]. In fact, when you consume excess sugar, many different components within your body feel the strain, which is bad news for your health in both the short and long term.

Eating sugar creates excess hormones such as dopamine and serotonin—an effect similar to cocaine consumption, which is highly addictive. Yeah, that's right! And like a drug, your body craves more after initial ingestion.

Another effect of sugar? Insulin spikes. Insulin facilitates absorption of glucose in the cells which leads to stabilization of sugar levels. Sugar can affect the way your insulin works, and once you experience a sugar crash, your blood sugar drops again. Sugar crashes and low blood sugar drain your energy and hinder your ability to perform daily tasks.

Artificial Sweeteners: Worse.

You may have already heard that artificial sweeteners are bad for you. But do you know exactly why? The FDA has five artificial sweeteners on its "approved" list: saccharin, aspartame, neotame, acesulfame, and sucralose.[2] While these sweeteners are legal, the human body and brain responds to these sweeteners in a very negative way.

Artificial sweeteners change the way food tastes, because they are sweeter and more potent than regular sugar or high-fructose corn syrup. Overconsumption of these sweeteners confuses your sugar receptors and limits your taste tolerance for foods that are not sweet. This means your body becomes less likely to tolerate foods that are less intense with their natural sweetness, such as fruit. Furthermore, food that is not sweet at all, like vegetables for example, become completely unpalatable.

---

2   FDA.org, "High Intensity Sweeteners," May 19, 2014.

Artificial sweeteners have another major disadvantage. Because they're zero calories, we think we can have as much as we want, and as a result, we start to crave sweets on a more frequent basis. We even tend to choose sweet food over nutritious food, which not only leads to weight gain, but also several other health problems.

Natural Sweeteners: The Best.
Natural sweeteners are not only a healthy alternative to sugar and artificial sweeteners, but they also allow you to choose a natural solution to sweeten your food. Use a liquid version of the sweetener if you are concerned about texture, but if not, a granular version works too. Natural sweeteners are non-addictive, which means you can have your cake and eat it too! Eating food made with one of the natural sweeteners below will help you slowly phase out your sugar addiction, and curb sweet cravings in the long run. Here's a list of some of my favorite sweeteners:

Agave Nectar
Agave has a low glycemic index, but a word to the wise—it's not the best natural sweetener. If you're craving sugar, it's better to use agave. There are, however, healthier options on this list.

Blackstrap Molasses
Blackstrap molasses is best in its pure, unsulfured form. It is rich in iron, calcium, and magnesium. It has a strong flavor, so use in small doses.

Brown Rice Syrup
Brown rice syrup raises your blood sugar without lowering your energy after intake. It breaks down in your system better because it is a complex carb, and when it comes to satisfying your sweet tooth, brown rice syrup can get the job done the natural way.

Coconut Nectar
Use this as a natural, healthy substitute for artificial sweeteners like processed sugar. Coconut nectar is a divine addition to many of the smoothies, sips, tonics, and dessert recipes in this book.

Coconut Sugar
You can also use coconut in its granulated form as coconut sugar. This is the ideal form of coconut sweetener for your desserts, coffee, or tea.

Pure Maple Syrup

This delicious sweetener is readily available, affordable, and is blender-friendly.

Stevia

An anti-inflammatory, natural, calorie-free herb, stevia is a powerful supplement for regulating bodily functions and increasing energy. It can be purchased in leaf form, powdered form, and liquid form. Stevia has a bitter aftertaste, so use in moderation.

Yacon Syrup

Yacon syrup is made from yacon roots and is sweet and dark with a molasses-like consistency. It is good for kidney and digestive disorders, so if you're experiencing those problems, yacon syrup is the natural sweetener for you.

Detox the Healthy Indulgence Way

It happened again. Overeating, partying, a hangover . . . you know how those activities make you feel. The feeling of sluggishness, lack of energy, and lack of enthusiasm make you feel like your body is out of sync with the time of day or with the types of tasks ahead of you. You want to face the day, but your body just won't cooperate. Additionally, if you have a poor diet, chances are that you are also suffering from a number of digestive issues, which is why you need to cleanse and detox your system, and eliminate excess by-products that have accumulated within your body. Incidentally, detoxification has been practiced for centuries by cultures all around the world (Greeks, Romans, Indians, Persians, Chinese, and Native Americans). Detoxing helps to feed your body with healthy nutrients to protect you from diseases, and preserves your health so you can function at an optimal level.

One important thing to remember is that there is a big difference between detoxing and juicing or going on a liquid diet. With *Sima's Healthy Indulgence*, I would never recommend going through a liquid cleanse or anything similar that shocks your system. My plan aims to help you detox in a gentle manner with results that are more profound and permanent. My detox process aims to cleanse and revamp your entire digestive system while naturally and smoothly restoring vitality to your intestines, kidneys, liver, and even your skin.

Key Elements in the Detox Process

Now that you know why detoxing is so important, we'll examine how to undergo a detox the Healthy Indulgence way. Below you will find a few of my personal recommendations to start your detox process.

1. Start your day with my warm power goji tea or with my turmeric latte (pages 203–206).
2. Eat breakfast, lunch, dinner, and a snack in between each. The point of this is to refresh and nourish yourself and not starve yourself. Cleansing can be enjoyable. Fasting, on the other hand, makes you want to gorge on everything in your kitchen. I recommend my morning smoothies, lunchtime soups or

salads, yummy snacks, a heavy-on-the-veggies dinner and a warm evening tea or my apple cinnamon water.

4. Make sure to drink plenty of water.

5. Take a break from coffee and alcohol. Don't worry, they will be there when you're done though you might realize that you may not want to renew that relationship.

6. Take a break from animal products.

7. Add probiotic foods to your diet. Probiotics are bacteria and I know what you're thinking—doesn't bacteria cause diseases? What you may not know is that there's two types of bacteria, good and bad, and probiotics are bacteria that are good for your metabolism and digestive system. Probiotics balance your body chemistry and help you digest your food properly. Some examples of probiotic foods include pickles, sauerkraut, low-dairy yogurt, and kombucha tea.

8. Add alkaline foods to your diet. An alkaline diet works to maintain the pH balance of fluids in your body at an optimum level. The more mineral-rich your food is, the better your pH balance will be. A healthy pH balance is important because it prevents most diseases and disorders from creating roots in your body. Fruits, nuts, legumes, and vegetables are examples of alkaline food.

9. Take some time to reflect and meditate. Take inventory and ask yourself important questions about yourself so you can successfully deal with any stress in your life.

This is my personal detox that I follow and have prescribed to hundreds of clients who have tested and proven it over the years, and I'm delighted to share it with you. At the end of this book, I have included a 3-day detox plan for you. I encourage you to come back to this plan whenever you feel your body is heavily saturated with unhealthy food or have been overindulging.

The Healthy Indulgence Kitchen

The Healthy Indulgence plan is all about crafting healthy, delicious meals for yourself and your family. In this section, you will learn more about the essentials that will help you on this important journey. If you remove unwanted temptations in your kitchen and have an organized space with easy access to all the items you need for this plan, you will find that your path to better nutrition is straightforward, enjoyable, and delicious.

Ready to begin? Let's start with a few simple steps to prepare your Healthy Indulgence kitchen.

Step 1: De-junk your kitchen

If you have anything in your freezer, pantry, or refrigerator that is refined, processed, or has ingredients that you can't pronounce, it's time to say good-bye and get them out of your kitchen. Cleaning the junk out of your refrigerator and pantry will make room for healthier and more nutritious foods.

Step 2: Give produce center stage

Adding fruits and vegetables to your daily menu is imperative and a big part of the Healthy Indulgence plan. These super nutrients can be added to your diet in the forms of juices, smoothies, salads, and soups, and you will find that fruits and vegetables play a big part in most of my recipes in this book.

Another advantage of adding vegetables and fruits to your diet is that you can also eat them raw, which means that you'll be getting the maximum amount of nutrients from your food.

Step 3: Clear out distractions

If you're constantly distracted while you're cooking, be it playing with your iPhone or watching TV, you are likely to botch your meal, use an incorrect amount of ingredients, and overall just not be very interested in what you're cooking. Getting rid of all the distractions around you while preparing and consuming your meal will lead to a healthier outlook when it comes to food and your own well-being.

Step 4: Infuse some zen into your kitchen

Don't just stop with clearing out the distractions. One study found that a relaxed environment increases satisfaction and decreases food consumption by around 18 percent, or roughly 175 calories[3]. So infuse some zen into your life by rearranging the design of your kitchen to make it feel welcoming to you and your guests. Try softening the lights, or putting on a little background music—whatever helps soothe your inner peace, and brings balance, calm, and happiness to your space.

Setting Up Your Kitchen

All-Purpose Grater

An all-purpose grater is good for grating citrus fruits to add that zesty flavor to dressings, sauces, and baked goods. You can also use the grater for garlic, onions, carrots, turmeric, ginger, and other veggies and fruits.

Cast-Iron Skillet

A cast-iron skillet is great for sautéing and stir-frying. It can be used both on the stovetop and in the oven.

Colander

A metal colander can serve multiple functions in a healthy kitchen. You can use it to rinse veggies or as a steam basket.

Food Processor

A food processor allows you to quickly mash garbanzo beans for hummus, or slice and grate veggies to make quick salads, salsas, and sauces.

Mason Jars

Mason jars are excellent for food storage and to take food on the go. They can be used to store smoothies, juices, granola, chia pudding, and salads.

Measuring Cups

A good measuring cup is essential to keep track of your portions.

---

3   *Cornell Chronicle*, Cornell University April 29, 2012.

Mixing Bowls

A set of mixing bowls—one small, one medium, and one large—are a great addition to your kitchen. Stainless steel is the best choice for your mixing bowls, but glass also works well.

Pots and Pans

Among the usual pots and pans, the most essential ones are a saucepan with a heavy lid, and a stockpot for soups.

Set of Knives

It's important to have a good set of knives in your kitchen. The most essential knives are the paring knife for dicing, the chef's knife for chopping meat and veggies, and the slicing knife for carving.

Spice Grinder

A coffee or spice grinder is perfect for grinding fresh spices, grains, coffee, nuts, and seeds.

Vitamix

A Vitamix is a must for your kitchen. If you're on a budget, a high-speed blender will do too. I recommend the Ninja, which costs only $80. You can use your blender to make many of my recipes such as smoothies, soups, crusts, cookies, coconut water, and even nice cream.

Wooden Cutting Board

A wooden cutting board is a must for chopping veggies, fruits, and for cutting fish, meat, and poultry. Wood is a better choice than glass or plastic because it is more sanitary in the long run.

Ingredient Essentials

In order to maximize your experience with this book, I've provided a list of simple ingredients you should have in the kitchen. These ingredients are easy to find, and they will help you prepare delectable recipes in the best way possible.

Pantry Items

OILS AND FRIENDLY FATS

- Avocado oil
- Coconut oil
- Sesame oil
- Raw tahini
- Cooking spray
- Extra-virgin olive oil

CONDIMENTS AND SAUCES

- Tabasco
- Dijon mustard
- Vegan mayo
- Harissa
- Sriracha

VINEGARS

- Apple cider vinegar
- Balsamic vinegar
- Red wine vinegar
- White wine vinegar

SWEETENERS

- Coconut nectar
- Pure maple syrup
- Coconut sugar
- Organic raw honey
- Pitted Medjool dates

BAKING

- Baking powder
- Whole vanilla bean
- Baking soda
- Dairy-free dark chocolate chips or chunks (70% cacao content or higher)
- Pure vanilla extract
- Unsweetened cacao/cocoa powder
- Whole vanilla bean

SPICES

- Black pepper
- Chili powder
- Dried rosemary
- Herbes de provence
- Saffron
- Za'atar spice blend
- Caraway seeds
- Curry powder
- Ground cinnamon
- Nutmeg
- Sea Salt
- Pink Himalayan salt
- Cayenne pepper
- Dried ginger
- Ground coriander
- Paprika, sweet or spicy
- Thyme
- Cinnamon sticks
- Dried oregano
- Ground cumin
- Red pepper flakes
- Turmeric powder

FLOURS

- Almond flour
- Coconut flour
- Whole wheat flour

OTHER PANTRY ITEMS

- Coconut milk (canned, full fat)
- Organic tomato sauce (no salt added)
- Organic tomato paste (no salt added)
- Quinoa flakes
- Organic broth
- Unsweetened applesauce
- Dairy-free protein powder

NUTS, SEEDS, AND SUPERFOODS

- Acai
- Coconut
  - Shredded
  - Oil
  - Water
- Goji berries
- Raw almonds
- Raw sunflower seeds
- Tahini
- Bee pollen
- Dates
- Hemp seeds
- Raw cashews
- Raw walnuts
- Wheat germ
- Cacao
  - Powder
  - Nibs
- Flaxseeds
- Pine nuts
- Raw hazelnuts
- Sesame seeds
  - Black
  - White
- Chia seeds
- Garlic
  - Black
  - White
- Pomegranate seeds
- Raw pistachios
- Spirulina

Fresh Ingredients

I cannot tell you to buy organic all the time, but I do recommend buying organic as much as possible.

My Favorite Fresh Ingredients

FRUITS

- Apples
- Cherries
- Kiwi
- Papaya
- Avocado
- Dragon fruit
- Lemon
- Pineapple
- Bananas
- Fresh figs
- Lime
- Pomegranate
- Berries
- Grapefruit
- Mango
- Oranges

VEGETABLES

- Asparagus
- Cauliflower
- Celery
- Bell peppers
- Broccoli
  - Sprouts
- Garlic
- Leafy Greens
  - Kale
  - Spinach
  - Romaine
  - Lettuce
  - Collard greens
  - Arugula
- Onions
- Radishes

- Ginger root
- Turmeric root
- Scallions
- Shallots
- Sweet lemons
- Sweet potatoes
- Tomatoes
- Yams
- Cucumbers

LOW LACTOSE DAIRY

- Feta cheese
- Goat cheese
- Greek yogurt
- Swiss cheese

HERBS

- Basil

- Cilantro
- Dill
- Mint
- Parsley
- Rosemary
- Thyme
- Tarragon

DAIRY-FREE

- Almond milk
- Cashew milk
- Coconut milk
- Coconut yogurt
- Kefir
- Unsweetened milks
  - Almond
  - Hemp
  - Quinoa

Meat, Poultry, Eggs, and Seafood

When looking for protein from animal sources and eggs, look for labels that include: grass-fed, pasture-raised, non-GMO, organic, soy-free, locally sourced, and sustainable.

MEAT & POULTRY

- Brisket
- Chicken
  - Whole
  - Deli slices
  - Ground
- Lean ground beef
- Turkey
  - Ground
  - Deli slices
  - Whole
- Fresh eggs

SEAFOOD

- Salmon
  - Fresh
  - Canned
- Tuna
  - Fresh
  - Canned (in water or olive oil)
- Ahi tuna
- Mahi mahi

The Healthy Indulgence Recipes

1. Each recipe in this book is PCF combo- (Protein, Carbs, Fats) approved, and all ingredients are measured for perfect portion sizes. Additionally, each recipe should take 30 minutes or less to prepare. I've already done most of the work for you, so all you have to do is choose your favorite recipes, prepare, indulge, and watch the pounds shrug off. Please note the number of servings indicated in each recipe—each serving is for one person. Notice also the superfood section in each recipe. Some are listed as optional, while some are part of the main ingredients in the recipe.

2. Each recipe is intended to have no more than *10 ingredients* and no more than *30 minutes* total time. However, the 10-ingredient count does not include the seasoning or spices. The 30-minutes is an approximation that will vary depending on your appliances, and does not include freezing or overnight refrigeration. I know how busy you all are and I have prepared these recipes to adhere to the 30-minute guidelines. But in case it takes you 37.452 minutes to make the recipe come out perfectly, then so be it.

3. Unless otherwise stated, always use the following ingredients when the recipe calls for them:
   - Olive oil → *extra-virgin olive oil*
   - Coconut oil → *raw cold-pressed extra-virgin unrefined coconut oil*
   - Eggs → *organic large cage-free eggs*
   - Cacao powder → *raw unsweetened 70% or more cacao*
   - Vegan option → *sub vegetable broth for chicken broth; sub coconut yogurt for Greek yogurt*

4. As you know, I'm not a fan of counting calories and the Healthy Indulgence plan doesn't ask you to do so. But if you want to have a rough idea of how many calories are present in each recipe, here's a breakdown:
   - Breakfast, Lunch, Dinner items: 300 – 400 calories per serving.
   - Snacks: 150 – 250 calories per serving.

5. Each recipe includes food allergen information on nuts, dairy, eggs, and also indicates which ones are vegan (or a vegan option is provided).

Sunrise

You've heard that "breakfast is the most important meal of the day," and it's absolutely true. When you wake up in the morning, you're coming out of a 6–8 hour fast, also known as your beauty sleep; your blood sugar is low and your body needs nutrients to wake it up. The best thing you can do for your body in the morning is to eat breakfast. For those of you who often skip breakfast, the recipes in this section will make you want to eat because you will gain the fuel and long-lasting energy to function during the day. This section of *Sima's Healthy Indulgence* gives you a few innovative recipes to start your day in confidence and will have you feeling like a champion in no time!

SUNRISE RECIPES

Rejuvenation Bowl

An alternative way to drink your smoothie is to have it as a smoothie bowl. They are great for breakfast, post-workout, or anytime as a snack. Having it in a bowl gives you the freedom to add a variety of superfoods and toppings arranged picture-perfect—because we all know we eat with our eyes. Feel free to use my optional superfood boosters or your own; I promise I won't be offended.

---

serves: 2

prep: 5 cook: 0 total: 5

dairy-free | egg-free | vegan

Ingredients
½ avocado

2 bananas (fresh or frozen)

1 cup mixed berries (fresh or frozen)

2 handfuls of spinach, kale, or collard greens

2 cups unsweetened nondairy milk of choice (almond, coconut, or hemp milk)

1 scoop protein powder, nondairy

2 tablespoons maple syrup or coconut nectar

1 teaspoon bee pollen

2 tablespoons raw almond butter

2 tablespoons unsweetened shredded coconut

Method
Combine all ingredients in a high-speed blender and blend on high for 1 to 2 minutes until all ingredients are mixed together. Then, pour into a bowl and add optional superfood boosts.

Sima's Tip
If you have a nut allergy, feel free to substitute your favorite seed butter instead. Hemp, and even sunflower butter are a great options.

Optional Superfoods
Per Serving

1 teaspoon raw sunflower seeds

1 tablespoon raw pistachios

1 teaspoon chia seeds

Rise and Shine Savory Muffins

There is nothing better than waking up to breakfast that is already prepared from the night before. With the house filled with the smell of peppers, eggs, and onions it's easy to wake up, get your day going, and handle anything that is thrown your way. So, go ahead and shine!

---

serves: 6
prep: 7 cook: 23 total:30
nut-free | dairy-free option: omit feta

Ingredients
6 large eggs
½ cup spinach (fresh or frozen)
½ cup tomatoes (diced)
¼ cup diced onion (or shallots)
½ cup crumbled low fat feta cheese
6 slices of 100% whole wheat toast

Method
Preheat oven to 350° and lightly grease a muffin pan. In a bowl, beat eggs and whisk until the yolk and whites are combined. Next, add the spinach, tomatoes, diced onions (or shallots), and feta cheese. Pour equal amounts of the egg mixture into the muffin pan. Bake for 23 minutes (the center of each muffin should be cooked through). Let cool for 2 minutes before serving with 100% whole wheat toast.

Optional Superfoods
Per Serving

1 teaspoon hemp seeds
1 teaspoon flaxseeds
1 teaspoon raw tahini

Powerhouse Huevos Rancheros

This is a wake-up call for your taste buds! With cilantro, jalapeños, and tomatoes, it will give you the power you need to take on the day. I dare you to try this, especially those of you who think out of the box and are willing to take a risk with something new and spicy (pile on the optional harissa and cayenne!).

serves: 2

prep: 10 cook: 20 total: 30

nut-free | dairy-free

Ingredients
1½ tablespoons olive oil
½ medium onion, chopped
2 medium tomatoes, fire-roasted, chopped
½ jalapeño pepper
½ teaspoon ground cumin (optional)
pinch of sea salt
pinch of black pepper
4 corn tortillas (or Ezekiel tortillas)
4 eggs
2 tablespoons cilantro, chopped
½ avocado, quartered
cooking spray

Method
Sauce: Sauté the onions and 1 tablespoon oil in a large skillet on medium heat. Once the onions are translucent, add chopped tomatoes and sauté until broken down. Add chopped jalapeño and cumin.

Tortillas: Heat ½ tablespoon of olive oil in skillet on medium high, coating the pan with the oil. Heat the tortillas in the pan until they are heated through, and they bubble up.

Eggs: On medium-high heat, spray skillet with cooking spray. Cook each egg individually, cooking for 3 to 4 minutes for runny yolks.

Assembly: Layer each tortilla with sauce, 1 egg, more sauce, cilantro, and ¼ avocado.

Sima's Tip
How to fire-roast a tomato: taking a tomato with a set of tongs, hold over the stove burner until tomato begins to blister and rotate until whole tomato is roasted.

Optional Superfoods
Per Serving

1 tablespoon pumpkin seeds
¼ teaspoon of cayenne pepper
1 teaspoon harissa

Breaking Bread Tartine

When I think of breaking bread, the first thing that comes to mind is home and family. There is a French inspired bakery/cafe chain called Le Pain Quotidien, which translates to "The Daily Bread." After trying their tartine dish, I was inspired to create this recipe. Tartine is an open-faced sandwich topped with your favorite ingredients. I hope that when you make it yourself, you get the same feeling of home and family.

serves 2
prep: 5 cook: 10 total: 15
egg-free | nut-free

Ingredients
4 slices 100% whole wheat
    bread or Ezekiel bread
4 oz goat cheese
2 cups arugula
4 eggs, sunny side up
    (cooked in spray)
1 medium avocado,
    quartered
1 teaspoon crushed pink
    peppercorns
½ teaspoon sea salt flakes

Method
First, toast bread in a toaster or skillet. Second, spread each slice of bread with goat cheese. Third, layer the arugula on the toast and top with an egg. Lastly, add avocado, crushed peppercorns, and sea salt flakes.

Note
For extra protein, add 1 slice of deli turkey meat per tartine. Omit peppercorn if sensitive to spice.

Optional Superfoods
Per Serving

¼ teaspoon ground
    turmeric
1 tablespoon toasted
    sesame seeds
1 teaspoon wheat germ

Have Your Pancakes and Eat Them Too

This recipe is ushering in a new era of pancakes that are no longer big stacks of carbs, but protein filled "pancakes" that fuel your day without all the heaviness of the traditional pancake. Using almond flour as an alternative to wheat flour makes it gluten-free, low in carbs, and high in protein. So, go ahead and enjoy these pancakes guilt-free!

serves: 4

prep: 10 cook: 10 total: 20

dairy-free | nut-free

Ingredients

2 cups old-fashioned oats
1½ cups vanilla almond milk
1½ large ripe bananas
1 teaspoon pure vanilla extract
1½ tablespoons maple syrup
½ teaspoon cinnamon
1 teaspoon lemon juice
1½ teaspoon baking powder
¼ teaspoon sea salt
1 egg
2 tablespoons melted coconut oil

Toppings

4 tablespoons maple syrup
4 cups fresh fruit (such as mixed berries, papaya, pineapple)

Method

First, add all the ingredients (except for egg and coconut oil) to a high-speed blender and blend for 2 minutes on medium-high (alternatively, you can add to a large bowl and whisk until all ingredients are mixed together). Then, add the egg and pulse until egg is completely mixed in. Heat a nonstick griddle to medium heat, add melted coconut oil, and after 30 seconds add the pancake batter, ¼ cup at a time. Cook for 2 minutes then flip the pancake and cook for another 2 minutes. Top off with maple syrup and fresh fruit.

Optional Superfoods

Per Serving

½ tablespoon maca powder
1 teaspoon unsweetened shredded coconut
½ teaspoon bee pollen

*Maca powder and bee pollen are not recommended for pregnant women or children.

Golden Mylk Chia Pudding

What's better than waking up in the morning and knowing something delicious is waiting for you in the fridge? A golden mylk or an overnight chocolate chia pudding. It's called golden mylk because of the great health benefits from combining turmeric and coconut milk. Boosting it with bee pollen, hemp seeds, and cacao nibs will give you the energy of the Hulk, without turning green or shredding your clothes. You've been warned.

serves: 2
prep: 5 cook: 5 total: 10
dairy-free | egg-free | nut-free option: replace almond milk with coconut milk
vegan option: omit bee pollen

Ingredients
2 cups unsweetened almond
    or coconut milk
½ teaspoon turmeric powder
½ teaspoon cinnamon
    powder
2 tablespoons maple syrup
4 tablespoons chia seeds

Method
In a saucepan add milk, turmeric powder, cinnamon, and maple syrup. Then, bring to a quick boil and simmer for 2 minutes. Strain into a bowl and add chia seeds. Lastly, pour into two separate containers or mason jars and refrigerate overnight.

Optional Superfoods
Per Serving

½ teaspoon bee pollen
1 teaspoon hemp seeds
½ tablespoon raw
    cacao nibs

Chocolate Chia Pudding

serves: 2
prep: 5 cook: 5 total: 10
dairy-free | egg-free | vegan | nut-free option: replace almond milk with coconut milk

Ingredients
2 cups of unsweetened
    almond or coconut milk
2 tablespoons cacao powder
½ teaspoon cinnamon
    powder
2 tablespoons maple syrup
4 tablespoons chia seeds

Method
In a saucepan add milk, cacao powder, cinnamon, and maple syrup. Then, bring to a quick boil and simmer for 2 minutes. Next, strain into a bowl and add chia seeds. Lastly, pour into two separate containers or mason jars and refrigerate overnight.

Optional Superfoods
Per Serving

1 date, chopped
2 teaspoons
    unsweetened
    shredded coconut
½ teaspoon maca
    powder

Green Tea Detox Smoothie

serves: 2
prep: 5 cook: 0 total: 5
dairy-free | egg-free | vegan

Ingredients	Method	Optional Superfoods
2 cups chilled green tea (unsweetened)	Combine all ingredients in high-speed blender and blend on high for 2–3 minutes. Pour into 2 tall glasses and top with optional superfood boosters.	Per Serving
2 cups chopped pineapples (fresh or frozen)		1 teaspoon spirulina
1 lemon (½ juiced + ½ whole lemon with skin)		1 teaspoon unsweetened shredded coconut
2 tablespoons grated ginger		1 teaspoon chia seeds
1 avocado		
2 scoops nondairy protein powder		
2 pitted Medjool dates		

Not Your Average Smoothie

Not all smoothies are created equal! By adding dragon fruit to your smoothie, your body will be enhanced with phytonutrients, antioxidants, and several B vitamins. It will set your body above the rest. It's Instagram-worthy, *for sure*. Snap away.

serves: 1
prep: 5 cook: 0 total: 5
egg-free | dairy-free | nut-free option: only if using water or coconut water | vegan

Ingredients	Method	Optional Superfoods
1 cup liquid (coconut water, hemp milk, quinoa milk, or almond milk)	Combine all ingredients in high-speed blender and blend on high for 2–3 minutes. Pour into 2 glasses and top with superfood boosters.	Per Serving
1 banana, frozen		1 teaspoon wheat germ
1 dragon fruit, peeled and chopped		1 teaspoon hemp seeds
1 scoop nondairy protein powder		1 teaspoon flaxseeds
1 Persian cucumber		
Juice of 1 lime		
½ apple		
1 pitted Medjool date		
¼ cup crushed ice		

Level-Up Porridge

If you need something to sustain you through the day, this warm power porridge is the solution to keep you going. It's almost like oatmeal, but elevated. I would encourage you to add the superfood boosters as they will level-up your breakfast experience.

serves: 1
prep: 0 cook: 25 total: 25
dairy-free | egg-free | vegan | nut-free option: replace almond milk with water

Ingredients
2 teaspoons coconut oil
½ cup uncooked quinoa
1¼ cups unsweetened almond milk (or any nondairy milk of choice)
½ teaspoon pure vanilla extract
¼ teaspoon ground cinnamon
1 pinch sea salt
1 whole Medjool date, diced

Method
In a sauce pot over medium heat, melt the coconut oil and add the quinoa; stir to coat. Let it sit for about a minute. Add the almond milk, vanilla, cinnamon, sea salt, and chopped date, and combine.

Bring up to a boil, then turn the heat down to a simmer for 10 minutes until the quinoa is cooked through and liquid has been absorbed. Cover and let stand for 10 minutes. Fluff with a fork before serving warm.

Optional Superfoods
Per Serving

2 teaspoons goji berries
1 teaspoon shredded unsweetened coconut
1 tablespoon pomegranate arils

Strawberry Rose Oatmeal

You must, must, *must*, try this layered oatmeal! It's warm, hearty, and I devour it every time I have it. The sweetness and all the superfoods in it make it a no-brainer for breakfast. Don't feel compelled to stick to one fruit, try any and all that are in season.

serves: 2
prep: 0 cook: 20 total: 20
dairy-free | egg-free | vegan

Ingredients
1 cup old-fashioned oats
½ teaspoon cinnamon
Pinch of sea salt
2½ cups unsweetened
    almond milk
1 scoop nondairy protein
    powder

Compote
2 cups fresh or frozen
    mixed berries
2 tablespoons water
1 tablespoon lemon juice
1 tablespoon coconut
    nectar or maple syrup
1 tablespoon rose water
1 tablespoon chia seeds

Note
You can use any fruit of
your choice (mangoes,
peaches, kiwi, or even figs.
Use fresh or frozen).

Method
Add oats, cinnamon, and sea salt to pot. Add nondairy milk and stir. Add in nondairy protein powder. Heat over medium-high heat for 8–10 minutes or until all the liquid has been absorbed. Be sure to stir the oats while cooking. Oatmeal is done when all the liquid is absorbed and the oats are thick and fluffy. Then, portion oats into two bowls, jars, or containers and serve with compote. Continue to layer oats and compote in your containers and top with fresh berries and optional superfood boosts.

For Compote
In a medium saucepan combine berries, water, lemon juice, sweetener, and rosewater over medium heat. Once the mixture has begun to defrost, add chia seeds and continue to cook over low to medium heat. After the mixture has softened, take a fork and mash berries to desired consistency.

Remove from heat and let stand for 15 minutes or until mixture has thickened and cooled.

Optional Superfoods
Per Serving

1 teaspoon popped
    amaranth
2 tablespoons goji
    berries
2 teaspoons
    pistachios

Skinny Beach Papaya Boats

Who wants to go on a tropical vacation? I do! Well, at least your taste buds will. These tropical fruit-filled papaya boats boost your fiber, potassium, and folate intake. If papaya is not your thing, feel free to switch to cantaloupe, pineapple, or watermelon—whatever floats your boat!

serves: 2
prep: 10 cook: 0 total: 10
nut-free | egg-free | dairy-free option: replace Greek yogurt with coconut yogurt

Ingredients
1 papaya, sliced in half
   lengthwise
1 cup dragon fruit, peeled
   and scooped into balls
½ cup blueberries
½ cup strawberries, sliced
1 cup 2% low-fat Greek
   yogurt, plain
2 teaspoons coconut nectar
   to drizzle
fresh mint leaves

Method
Cut papaya in half, lengthwise. Then remove seeds and fill with fruit and yogurt. Lastly, drizzle with coconut nectar and add mint leaves.

Optional Superfoods
Per Serving

1 teaspoon lacuma powder
1 teaspoon raw unsweetened
   shredded coconut
1 teaspoon raw cacao nibs

Your Kind of Granola Bars

Forget about those store-bought, sugar-laden granola bars! Here to save the day are your own homemade bars. Best part about them is that they are totally customizable to you and your taste buds with no artificial ingredients. Grab your family and get your hands dirty to make these delicious treats—your kids will thank you for it!

serves: 8 (1 bar per person)
prep: 5 cook: 25 total: 30
dairy-free | egg-free | vegan

Ingredients
1 cup old-fashioned rolled oats
½ cup uncooked quinoa
2 tablespoons pumpkin seeds
1 tablespoon sesame seeds
2 tablespoons dried cherries (or any dried fruit of your choice)
½ cup unsweetened nut or seed butter
pinch of sea salt
¼ cup pure maple syrup
1 teaspoon pure vanilla extract
1 tablespoon coconut oil

Method
Preheat oven to 350°. Add oats, quinoa, and pumpkin seeds to a large baking sheet and spread evenly. Bake the oats and quinoa mixture for 10 minutes. When done, transfer to a large bowl, add the sesame seeds and dried cherries and set aside. Next, in a medium saucepan over low heat, add the almond butter (or your favorite nut or seed butter), sea salt, maple syrup, vanilla extract, and coconut oil. Stir until the mixture becomes creamy. Remove from heat and let cool for 5 minutes. Add the almond butter mixture to the oats and quinoa mixture and stir well. Line a 9x5 baking pan with parchment paper and pour granola mixture on top. Spread evenly and press down with your hands. Freeze for 10–15 minutes (granola mixture will harden).

Remove from freezer and cut into 8 bars.

Sima's Tips
To keep fresh, store them in the fridge or freezer.

If you have a nut allergy feel free to substitute your favorite seed butter instead. Hemp, and even sunflower butter are a great options.

Optional Superfoods
Per Serving

1 teaspoon pumpkin seeds (included in recipe)
1 teaspoon sunflower seeds
1 pinch cinnamon

Almond Oats To-Go

If you want to get in those extra 10 minutes of shut-eye in the morning, I highly recommend making these oats overnight. This will allow you to get your beauty rest and have a breakfast of champions without putting in the work in the morning. Go ahead, hit that snooze button one more time, I got you covered!

serves: 4
prep: 5 cook: 0 total: 5
egg-free | dairy-free | vegan

Ingredients
2 cups quick-cooking oats
½ teaspoon sea salt, divided into four
4 teaspoons maple syrup or coconut nectar
2 cups unsweetened vanilla almond milk (or nondairy milk of your choice), divided
1 teaspoon pure vanilla extract, divided into four
½ cup raw almonds, sliced

Method
In four mason jars, divide ¼ cup of the oats into each, along with the sea salt and your choice of sweetener. Add ½ cup vanilla almond milk and vanilla extract into each jar. Stir until mixed well. Add sliced almonds and close jars with lids. Refrigerate jars for at least 2 hours or overnight.

Optional Superfoods
Per Serving

1 teaspoon cinnamon
1 teaspoon bee pollen
1 teaspoon lucuma powder

Jerusalem Shakshuka

When I talk to my clients about shakshuka, they always do a double take and say "What?" It is an Israeli dish made with eggs, tomato sauce, and spices. In Israel, it is usually eaten for breakfast, but I must confess I find myself eating it at any given time of the day. It is a signature dish in my home and even better than that, you can make it your own custom dish by adding your own favorite toppings. Anything goes: tomatoes, turkey bacon, feta cheese, or even sweet potatoes. Simple yet very delicious!

serves: 3
prep: 10 cook: 15 total: 25
nut-free | dairy-free: omit feta

Ingredients

2 tablespoons olive oil
1 medium onion, peeled and diced
3 garlic cloves, minced
1 small red bell pepper, chopped
3 cups ripe diced tomatoes
1 tablespoon tomato paste
3 tablespoons water
1 teaspoon cumin
1 teaspoon paprika
pinch of cayenne pepper (or more if you like it spicy)
pinch of sea salt and black pepper
6 medium eggs

Optional

1 sliced jalapeño and 3 ounces low fat crumbled feta cheese

Method

Heat a deep, large skillet on medium heat. Add olive oil to the pan. Add diced onion, and sauté for a few minutes until the onion begins to brown and get a golden color. Add the garlic and continue to sauté for 2 minutes. Add the chopped bell pepper; sauté for additional 3 minutes. Then, in a small bowl mix together the tomatoes, tomato paste, spices, and 3 tablespoons of water. Stir with a fork and add the tomato mixture to the hot skillet. Let it cook for 5 minutes on medium heat until it starts to reduce. Next, crack the eggs into the skillet and season with sea salt and pepper. Reduce to low heat, cover the pan, and let it cook for 12–15 more minutes (to prevent from burning, make sure sauce does not reduce too much). Remove from heat and garnish with optional jalapeño and feta cheese.

Sima's Tip

Shakshuka can be eaten for breakfast, lunch, or dinner. Serve with 100% whole wheat warm crusty bread or 100% whole wheat pita bread that can be dipped into the sauce.

Optional Superfoods
Per Serving

cayenne pepper (included in recipe)
jalapeño (included in recipe)
1 black garlic clove, minced

Sandwiches

In this
section of *Sima's Healthy
Indulgence*, you'll find a new and original
approach to sandwich-making. Each recipe leads to a
delicious sandwich or wrap that will satisfy your hunger and is
embedded with the perfect combination of PCF: protein, carbs, and
fat that your body needs! Here you'll find some of my clients' favorites
like Napa Chicken Sandwich and Za'atar Chickpea Pocket. Each recipe is
a complete meal, ideal for lunch or brunch, whichever you prefer. A good
thing to remember is that not all breads are created equal. Try to stay away
from white bread or any bread that contains refined flour. For a healthier
alternative, choose 100% whole wheat bread because it tastes just as
good and is better for you. So, come on in to my kitchen and
let's break some bread together.

SANDWICHES RECIPES

Salmon That Burger

If you're like me and need a little variety in your food, switch it up from your regular meat patty and try a salmon burger. I am a big fan of making things from scratch, but sometimes even I need some help! So for this recipe I opted for a pre-made salmon burger. But, the added cauliflower spread is a unique way to ramp up your sandwich and add a non-traditional twist to your meal. So go ahead and break tradition!

serves: 4 (1 per person)
prep: 5 cook: 20 total: 25
nut-free | egg-free | dairy-free

Cauliflower spread
4 cups cauliflower (about half a head), chopped or blended into 1-inch florets
⅓ cup olive oil, + 2 tablespoons for roasting
2 teaspoons herbs de Provence
1 black garlic clove
2 tablespoons lemon juice
½ teaspoon sea salt
¼ teaspoon black pepper

Ingredients
4 100% whole wheat buns
Cauliflower spread (recipe above)
4 frozen salmon burgers (found at your local health food store), defrosted and prepared to your liking
2 cups arugula
8 watermelon radishes, sliced
2 medium tomatoes, sliced

Method

Cauliflower spread
Toss cauliflower florets with 2 tablespoons of olive oil. Lay out the cauliflower in a single layer on a baking pan and roast at 400° until tender and starting to brown, about 18 minutes. Place the roasted cauliflower and the rest of the ingredients in a high-speed blender or food processor and process until smooth.

Take bottom part of the wheat bun and layer with 2 tablespoons of the cauliflower spread, followed by the salmon patty, ½ cup of arugula, radishes, a tomato slice, and more cauliflower spread. Top with top part of the bun.

Optional Superfoods
Per Serving

¼ avocado per burger
½ teaspoon crushed sunflower seeds
black garlic (included in recipe)

The Kabob to My Naan

If you love to barbeque and have a good time with your friends and family, this recipe is the reason to invite people over and have a party. The addition of mint and cilantro to the kabob will completely upgrade your normal, everyday chicken! Put these kabobs on the grill, blast that music, and go enjoy the outdoors with your loved ones!

serves: 4
prep: 15 cook: 10 total: 25
nut-free | egg-free | dairy-free

Ingredients
100% whole wheat Naan Bread

Kabob
1 pound lean ground chicken
⅓ cup sliced scallions
⅓ cup chopped mint
4 tablespoons chopped cilantro
3 garlic cloves, finely chopped
1 teaspoon ground cumin
1 teaspoon ground coriander
1½ teaspoons sea salt
2 tablespoons raw tahini
4 medium wooden skewers

Salad
1½ green onions, thinly sliced
2 cups cherry tomatoes, halved
4 Persian cucumbers, sliced
¼ cup fresh mint leaves
¼ cup fresh parsley

Dressing
4 teaspoons ground sumac
3 tablespoons fresh lemon juice
1 tablespoon pomegranate
 molasses
2 small garlic cloves, minced
4 tablespoons extra-virgin olive
 oil
pinch of sea salt

Method

For the Kabob
Put all ingredients (except the skewers) into a large bowl and mix together. Divide the mixture into 4 parts and then with damp hands, shape around 4 soaked skewers (it should resemble a "hot-dog shape"). Heat a grill pan or regular pan to medium high, brush the kabobs with a bit of oil, and cook for 8–10 minutes on each side or until cooked through.

For the Salad
Toss all ingredients together in a large bowl.

For the Dressing
In a small bowl, add sumac, lemon juice, molasses, garlic, and olive oil. Whisk to combine and season with sea salt. Next, combine the dressing with the salad and toss until lightly dressed. Place spoonful of salad on toasted whole wheat naan and top with kabobs and drizzle with more dressing. Wrap and serve warm.

Optional Superfoods
Per Serving

1 tablespoon
 sesame seeds
1 tablespoon hemp
 seeds
2 tablespoons
 sunflower seeds

Za'atar Chickpea Pocket

Za'atar is a spice mix that is prominent in Mediterranean cuisine. It consists of dried thyme, oregano, marjoram, sesame seeds, and salt. It can be used in many different recipes like meat, vegetables, or even on sandwiches. This sandwich recipe in particular is delicious, colorful, and a great combination of Mediterranean flavors that will melt in your mouth and give you just the right amount of fullness.

serves: 2 (1 per person)
prep: 12 cook: 3 total: 15
egg-free | nut-free | dairy-free | vegan

Ingredients

Filling

2 radishes
2 Persian cucumbers
1 medium tomato
6 kalamata olives
½ cup broccoli sprouts
½ cup low sodium chickpeas
1 tablespoon za'atar
1 tablespoon white sesame
  seeds
2 100% sprouted whole
  grain pita bread

Tahini Sauce
½ cup raw tahini
1 clove minced garlic (more
  if you like garlicky)
juice of half a lemon
pinch of sea salt
¼ cup water (add more if
  needed)

Method
Slice radishes, cucumbers, tomatoes, and olives. Warm chickpeas with za'atar and sesame seeds on medium-high heat for 3–5 minutes, and stir until thoroughly coated. In a bowl, mix together the tahini, garlic, lemon, and salt, and set aside. Stuff pita with veggies and chickpeas, and top off with tahini sauce. Wrap and serve.

Optional Superfoods
Per Serving

pinch cayenne pepper
white sesame seeds (in tahini)
1 teaspoon black sesame seeds

Chicken Wrap with a Kick

If you're looking for a chicken wrap that will not only make your tummy happy, but will also boost your metabolism and help you burn more calories, look no further! The highlighting ingredient in this wrap is harissa, a hot chili pepper paste from Tunisia that consists of roasted red peppers, serrano peppers, hot chili peppers, and spices. Harissa is not your average type of chili paste so it'll add a new and vibrant flavor to the recipe. Get ready and let's kick those calories away!

serves: 2

prep: 12 cook: 0 total: 12

egg-free | dairy-free option: omit yogurt sauce | nut-free option: omit almonds

Ingredients

Chicken
2 teaspoons harissa
pinch of cayenne pepper
⅛ teaspoon cinnamon
pinch of sea salt
⅛ teaspoon allspice
2 (4) ounces chicken breasts,
   cooked, chopped, and
   warmed

Wrap
½ cup spinach leaves
2 100% whole wheat tortillas
4 tablespoons sliced raw
   almonds

Sauce
¼ cup 2% plain Greek yogurt
1 teaspoon fresh lemon juice

Method

In a medium bowl, whisk together the harissa, cayenne, cinnamon, sea salt, and allspice. Add the chopped chicken and toss well to coat. Arrange ¼ cup of spinach leaves in the center of each tortilla (leave room around the edges), place 1 chicken breast over the spinach and then sprinkle 2 tablespoons of sliced almonds on top. Mix together the yogurt and fresh lemon juice. Drizzle half of the sauce over each wrap and then roll the wrap tightly and slice in half or diagonally.

Sima's Tip
If you don't like it spicy, feel free to omit the harissa sauce and cayenne pepper.

Optional Superfoods

Per Serving

cayenne
   (included in recipe)
cinnamon
   (included in recipe)
1 teaspoon sunflower
   seeds

Skinny Minny Meatballs

Everyone has their own rendition for skinny meatballs, but my recipe is different from the rest. My addition of dates to the sauce brings in the sweetness needed to balance the acidity in the tomatoes and a unique flavor. So go ahead, be different. It will look good on you.

serves: 4 (makes 16 meatballs; 4 per person)
prep: 10 cook: 20 total: 30
dairy-free | nut-free

Ingredients

1¼ pounds lean ground beef
1 teaspoon sea salt
½ teaspoon dry oregano
½ teaspoon paprika, sweet or spicy
1 large egg, lightly beaten
½ cup quick-cooking rolled oats
1 clove garlic, finely chopped
¼ cup parsley, finely chopped
4 slices 100% sprouted whole grain
    bread
nonstick cooking spray

Marinara Sauce

2 cans (14.5 oz) fire roasted
    tomatoes
½ cup fresh basil leaves, loosely
    packed
1 clove garlic
2 pitted Medjool dates (optional)
10 oil-packed sun dried tomato,
    halves (optional)
2 tablespoons fresh lemon juice
¼ cup extra-virgin olive oil
½ teaspoon sea salt
¼ teaspoon black pepper
2 teaspoons apple cider vinegar
    (with "the mother")

Method

Preheat oven to 400°. Lightly coat large baking sheet with spray and set aside. Combine ground beef, salt, oregano, paprika, egg, oats, garlic, and parsley in large bowl. Mix well by hands (don't overmix, otherwise it will become too dense). Roll mixture into 16 1-inch meatballs and place on baking sheet with enough space between each meatball. Then bake for 20–25 minutes, or until no longer pink in the middle and browned on the outside. Top each bread slice with 4 skinny meatballs and drizzle 3 tablespoons of marinara sauce on top.

Marinara Sauce

Add all ingredients to a high-speed blender and blend until smooth. Warm on medium heat for 3-5 minutes prior to serving. Will stay fresh refrigerated in an airtight container for 2–3 days.

Optional Superfoods

Per Serving

apple cider vinegar
    (included in recipe)
1 teaspoon flaxseeds
½ teaspoon cayenne
    pepper

Asian Persuasion Burger

Do you love turkey burgers? I sure do! This turkey burger recipe is packed with wonderful flavor and is a healthy indulgence as well. By adding oats, you consume fiber and increase its health benefits. Also, my addition of Asian-inspired coleslaw will give the burger a unique twist and a burst of flavor. What are you waiting for? Have I persuaded you yet to try this recipe?

serves: 3
prep: 20 cook: 10 total: 30
nut-free | dairy-free

Ingredients
3 100% whole wheat hamburger
  buns (or Ezekiel buns)
1 tablespoon olive oil
3 tablespoons Mayonaiz-ey (see
  recipe on page 177)
1 teaspoon sriracha sauce

Turkey Burgers
1 large egg
1 pound lean ground turkey
¼ cup ground instant oats
½ cup chopped red onions
1 tablespoon low sodium soy sauce
1 tablespoon lime juice
1 tablespoon coconut sugar
½ teaspoon each: sea salt, dried
  basil, garlic powder
¼ teaspoon ground ginger
pinch of ground black pepper

Asian Slaw
3 cups chopped white cabbage
¾ cup matchstick carrots
2–3 tablespoons apple cider vinegar
  (with "the mother")
juice of 1 lime
1 tablespoon olive oil
1 teaspoon coconut nectar

Method

Turkey Burgers
Add egg to a large bowl and gently whisk. Add all remaining hamburger ingredients and mix with your hands until thoroughly combined. Form mixture into 3 equal patties roughly the size of the hamburger buns. Refrigerate for 15 minutes. In a small bowl, whisk together Mayonaiz-ey sauce and sriracha sauce.

Asian Slaw
In another bowl, add chopped cabbage and carrots and toss with vinegar, lime juice, olive oil, and coconut nectar. Refrigerate.

Heat 1 tablespoon of olive oil in a large skillet over medium-high heat. Once hot, add patties and cook for about 5 minutes or until brown and slightly charred on one side. Flip, reduce heat to medium, and cover. Cook an additional 3–5 minutes or to desired doneness and place on bottom buns. Top patties with slaw. Lastly, spread each bun top with 2 tablespoons Mayonaiz-ey and sriracha mixture; place atop burgers and Asian slaw.

Optional Superfoods
Per Serving

2 teaspoons
  sesame seeds
1 oz fresh ginger,
  grated
1 tablespoon
  edamame

Malibu Beach Tarragon Egg Salad

Do you ever eat something that reminds you of a relaxing day at the beach? This tarragon egg salad will be just that! The addition of tarragon livens up the regular egg salad and gives it an aroma that is so enticing you'll keep on wanting more. It's a staple to have prepared in the fridge so it's ready to go whenever you want to head to the beach!

serves: 2
prep: 5 cook: 10 total: 15
nut-free | dairy-free

Ingredients
4 whole hard boiled eggs +
    2 egg whites (you don't
    want too much yolk),
    chopped
¼ cup vegan mayo (or easy
    Mayonaiz-ey sauce recipe
    on page 177)
2 green onions, chopped
¼ cup chopped tarragon
½ teaspoon sea salt
½ teaspoon black pepper
4 slices 100% whole wheat
    bread, toasted

Method
In a large bowl, combine hard boiled eggs, mayo sauce, green onions, tarragon, sea salt, and black pepper.

Serve on toasted 100% whole wheat bread.

Sima's Tip
Alternatively, have the egg salad on a sweet potato round and have it as a Healthy Indulgence-approved snack. You can also serve with pickles on the side; it is my favorite addition to this sandwich!

Optional Superfoods
Per Serving

pinch black sesame
    seeds
pinch cayenne pepper
½ teaspoon hemp seed
    powder

Change My Life Lox Wrappers

This gorgeous sweet potato and lox wrapper recipe is hashtag delicious! They come loaded with omega-3 fatty acids, which is the "good fat" and can be found in the lox. Keep in mind that your body cannot make this fat and you can only obtain it through food like fish. By consuming these wrappers, it will not only be a great health benefit for you but it will definitely change your life!

serves: 8
prep: 15 cook: 10 total: 25
nut-free | egg-free | dairy-free

Ingredients

1 medium sweet potato
8 rice paper rounds
1 large Hass avocado (⅛th per roll)
8 oz lox
2 Persian cucumbers, julienned
½ bunch of cilantro
2 watermelon radishes, thinly sliced

Method

Cut the sweet potato into 8 ¼-inch slices, place in the oven, and roast at 400° for 10 minutes, then set aside. Fill a large bowl with room temperature water. Working with one rice paper wrapper at a time, dip into the water so the entire wrapper is submerged. Once it is thoroughly soaked, remove from the water and lay it on your work surface (the rice paper wrapper will be fairly stiff, but it will continue to soften as you work). Next, arrange some of the avocado slices in the center bottom of the wrapper. Then top with the lox, cucumber, sweet potato, cilantro, and radish. Fold each side of the wrapper to the center and tightly roll up from the bottom so it is secure. Serve and enjoy!

Optional Superfoods

Per Serving

¼ teaspoon hemp seeds
¼ teaspoon sesame seeds
¼ teaspoon sunflower seeds

Napa Chicken Sandwich

People go to Napa for the wine as this region has some of the best wines in the world. I went for the olives! I was inspired by my trip and was compelled to create a recipe because of it. The combination of olive tapenade and roasted pepper in this sandwich is delightful, but the black garlic makes it scrumptious. So mellow out with your favorite bottle of wine and bite into this delectable sandwich!

serves: 2
prep: 10 cook: 0 total: 10
nut-free | egg-free | dairy-free

Olive Tapenade
(makes about ½ cup)
8 oz pitted and minced
    kalamata olives
2 black garlic cloves, minced
1 white garlic clove, minced
2 teaspoons capers, rinsed and
    drained
2 teaspoons Italian parsley,
    chopped
1 teaspoon lemon zest
pinch of sea salt
pinch of black pepper
2 tablespoons extra-virgin
    olive oil

Ingredients
2 4-oz each boneless, skinless
    grilled chicken breast
4 slices sprouted 100% whole
    grain bread
6 roasted red pepper slices
    (store bought)
4 tablespoons olive tapenade
    (recipe below)
1 cup arugula

For Olive Tapenade
Add all ingredients to a high-speed blender and blend until mixed together.

Method

Place 2 bread slices on cutting board. Spread each bread slice with 3 tablespoons of your fresh olive tapenade. Cut chicken breasts into slices and arrange on each slice. Layer 3 slices of red peppers and ½ cup arugula.

Optional Superfoods
Per Serving

black garlic (in tapenade)
½ teaspoon hemp seeds
½ teaspoon wheat germ

Not-So-Guilty Grilled Cheese

I love taking ordinary comfort food, like grilled cheese sandwiches, and giving it my Healthy Indulgence makeover. As you know, I don't include much dairy in my plan, but Swiss cheese is one of my choices—a single slice provides 7 grams of protein. So go ahead and enjoy this guilty pleasure, minus the guilt.

---

serves: 2 (1 sandwich per person)
prep: 5 cook: 15 total: 20
egg-free | nut-free

Ingredients
3 teaspoons olive oil
1 medium onion, chopped
5 ounces mushrooms, chopped (any kind)
pinch of sea salt
4 slices low fat Swiss cheese
4 slices 100% whole wheat bread or Ezekiel bread
coconut oil spray

Method
In a skillet over medium-high heat, add 2 teaspoons of olive oil. When oil is hot, add the onion and cook until dark brown in color and softened; remove from heat and set aside. Add the remaining teaspoon of olive oil to the skillet and add the mushrooms and pinch of sea salt. Cook the mushrooms about 5 minutes until softened. Set aside. Spray the skillet with coconut oil and brown 2 slices of bread for about 2 minutes per side. Once the bread is browned, add a slice of cheese to each slice and let melt. Place caramelized onions on one slice of bread, then the mushrooms on top, and top with another slice of bread. Slice sandwiches in half and indulge!

Optional Superfoods
coconut oil (already in recipe)
¼ avocado per sandwich
1 pinch of cayenne pepper

Red Carpet—Ready Lentil Burger

This meatless burger is a great healthy alternative to eating a burger, without sacrificing flavor. Lentils may be tiny, but they pack a punch and come with health benefits like soluble fiber, which helps stabilize your blood sugar levels. Serve this vegetarian burger with sweet potato "fries" and dig in! You'll be ready to walk down that red carpet with full confidence.

serves: 4

prep: 15 cook: 15 total: 30

egg-free | dairy-free

Ingredients

Red Carpet Lentil Burger

4 tablespoons olive oil
1 large yellow onion, chopped
1 cup mushrooms, chopped
  (such as cremini)
3 garlic cloves, minced
1 teaspoon sea salt
pinch of black pepper
1 cup green lentils, cooked and
  drained
1 egg, beaten
½ cup 100% whole wheat
  bread crumbs
¼ cup leeks, chopped (optional)
2 tablespoons sunflower seeds,
  chopped
1 teaspoon Dijon mustard
1 teaspoon paprika
buns

Extras

4 leaves butter lettuce
4 slices heirloom tomatoes
4 slices red onions

Mayo

see no-egg- Mayonaiz-ey
  recipe on page 177

Method

In a large skillet over medium-high heat, add 2 tablespoons of olive oil and sauté onion and mushrooms until translucent, about 5 minutes. Add garlic, sea salt, and black pepper and sauté for another minute. Turn heat off, remove from heat, and set aside to cool. In a large bowl, mix in the rest of the ingredients, then add the onion-mushroom mixture and mix gently until all ingredients are thoroughly combined. Add a bit more bread crumbs if the mixture feels too wet or too sticky. Divide your burger mixture into 4 patties. In a large skillet over medium heat, add remaining 2 tablespoons olive oil, add the patties, and fry until golden brown in color, about 5 minutes on each side. Remove from heat. Build your lentil burger by spreading 1 tablespoon of Mayonaiz-ey over bottom of a toasted bun, a leaf of butter lettuce, slice of tomato, lentil burger, a slice of red onion, and the top bun spread with another tablespoon of Mayonaiz-ey.

Sima's Tip:

Eliminate bun, wrap with lettuce, and serve with sweet potato "fries."

Optional Superfoods

Per Serving

sunflower seeds
  (included in
  recipe)
¼ avocado
1 clove of black
  garlic (mash and
  add to mayo)

Tahini Turkey Sandwich

This is an absolutely gorgeous sandwich with just a few ingredients including turkey, tahini, and sprouts. What I love about this sandwich is that the broccoli sprouts provide only 5 grams of carbs, with 2 grams of protein and 4 grams of fiber, and contain sulforaphane, a powerful plant chemical with many health benefits. Not only will you have a mouthful of deliciousness but also a body full of goodness!

---

serves: 2
prep: 10 cook: 0 total: 10
nut-free | egg-free | dairy-free

Ingredients
4 slices 100% whole
    wheat bread
2 tablespoons raw
    tahini
½ avocado, quartered
1 ripe tomato, sliced
8 leaves of lettuce
4 slices turkey bacon,
    cooked
2 handfuls broccoli
    sprouts

Method
Lightly spray olive or coconut oil in a skillet or toaster and toast bread. Once the bread is toasted, place bread on cutting board and spread tahini on toast. Then layer with avocado, tomato, and lettuce. Top with 2 bacon slices per sandwich. Finish with a handful of broccoli sprouts on top. Serve and enjoy.

Optional Superfoods
1 teaspoon chia seeds
broccoli sprouts
    (included in recipe)
tahini (included in
    recipe)

Soups & Salads

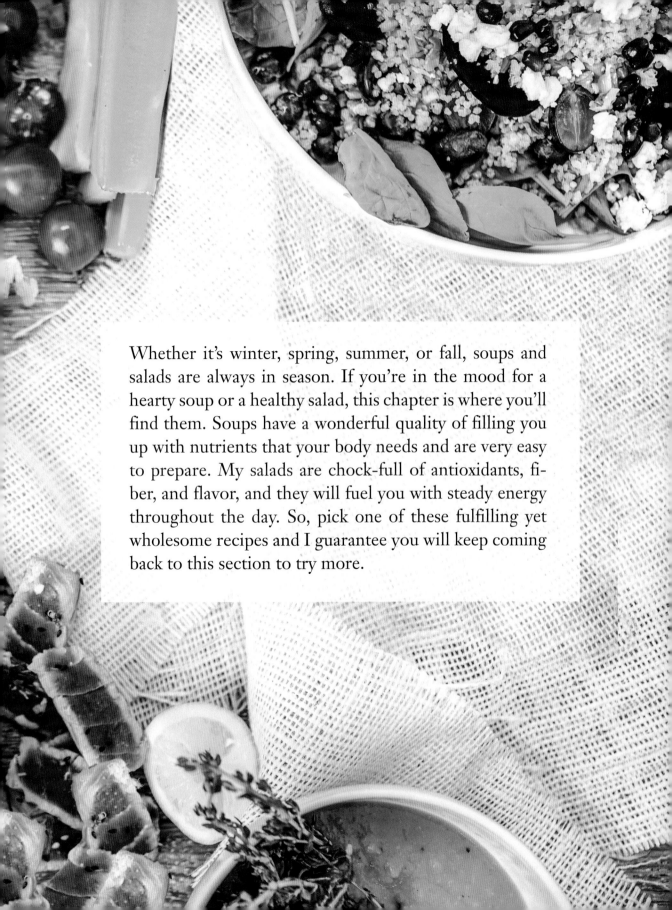

Whether it's winter, spring, summer, or fall, soups and salads are always in season. If you're in the mood for a hearty soup or a healthy salad, this chapter is where you'll find them. Soups have a wonderful quality of filling you up with nutrients that your body needs and are very easy to prepare. My salads are chock-full of antioxidants, fiber, and flavor, and they will fuel you with steady energy throughout the day. So, pick one of these fulfilling yet wholesome recipes and I guarantee you will keep coming back to this section to try more.

SOUPS & SALADS RECIPES

Happy and Sweet Soup

Sweet potatoes are AH-mazing. With this recipe, your tummy will not only be happy, but healthy as well. Sweet potatoes are inexpensive, delicious, and provide a world of benefits. They regulate your blood sugar (low glycemic index), are loaded with fiber making you feel full, and are ultra-rich in beta-carotene, a substance that has the ability to stave off cancer. My addition of turmeric to this soup will add extra flavor and even more health benefits.

serves: 2

prep: 5 cook: 25 total: 30

egg-free | dairy-free | vegan

Ingredients
1 tablespoon coconut oil
1 medium onion, chopped
1¾ teaspoons turmeric powder
1 teaspoon coriander, ground
pinch of cinnamon and sea salt
1 tablespoon raw turmeric, grated
¾ pound sweet potatoes, peeled and chopped
½ cup red lentils
2 cups vegetable broth
2 cups water
⅓ cup coconut milk
juice from 1 small lemon
2 pieces 100% whole wheat naan bread

Method
Heat a large pot over medium heat and add the coconut oil. Allow to melt and add the chopped onion. Sauté for 5–6 minutes until translucent. Stir in the turmeric powder, ground coriander, sea salt, cinnamon, and raw turmeric, and let it cook for 2 minutes. Add the chopped sweet potatoes, lentils, broth, and water. Bring to a boil, reduce to a simmer, and let it cook until everything becomes soft (about 20 minutes). Remove from heat and pour into high-speed blender and blend on high for 3–4 minutes. Add lemon juice and coconut milk, and serve warm with naan bread.

Optional Superfoods
Per Serving

turmeric (in recipe)
cinnamon (in recipe)
1 tablespoon walnuts, chopped

Overindulgent Weekend Detox Soup

This soup is refreshing, light, and will keep you feeling full and energized. It can be an everyday staple or a recovery soup after an overindulgent weekend.

serves: 4
prep: 5 cook: 25 total: 30
egg-free | nut-free | dairy-free | vegan

Ingredients
2 tablespoons olive oil
1 medium onion, diced
2 garlic cloves, chopped
1 (15-oz) can low sodium cannellini beans, drained and rinsed
½ cup white quinoa
7 cups vegetable broth
2½ cups chopped kale
1 teaspoon sea salt
½ teaspoon ground black pepper

Method
Heat olive oil in a large saucepan over medium-high heat. Add onion and cook about 5 minutes, until translucent. Add chopped garlic, beans, quinoa, and broth. Bring to a boil, then stir in kale. Season with salt and pepper. Reduce heat, partially cover, and simmer about 20 minutes.

Optional Superfoods
Per Serving

garlic (included in recipe)
¼ avocado
¼ teaspoon raw, grated ginger

Weekday Earth Detox Soup

serves: 4
prep: 5 cook: 25 total: 30
egg-free | dairy-free | nut-free option: omit pine nuts

Ingredients
2 heads of broccoli (including stems)
2 garlic cloves, chopped
pinch of sea salt
pinch of ground black pepper
2 tablespoons olive oil
1 medium onion, diced
3 cups vegetable broth
(15-oz) can low sodium cannelloni beans
⅓ cup coconut milk
4 lime wedges (optional)

Method
Preheat oven to 400°. Chop the broccoli (save the stems!) into florets and place on a baking sheet with garlic, salt, pepper, and 1 tablespoon olive oil and roast for 15 minutes. Meanwhile, peel the broccoli stems and chop into small pieces. Heat the remaining olive oil over medium heat. Add the onions and broccoli stems, cover, and cook for 5 minutes. Add broth and beans, cover, turn heat to low, and simmer for 15 minutes. Add the roasted broccoli and garlic to the saucepan and stir all ingredients together. Transfer to a high-speed blender and blend until smooth. Return to the saucepan and add the coconut milk. Garnish with lime wedges and serve warm.

Optional Superfoods
Per Serving

1 teaspoon sunflower seeds
1 teaspoon pine nuts
garlic (included in recipe)

Sima's Tip
When using a bunch of kale, remove the center stem and chop the leaves. You can substitute cannellini beans with garbanzo beans and switch spinach or swiss chard instead of kale.

Orange Velvet Soup

This is a luxuriously delicious soup. The combination of coconut milk and red lentils lends itself to a smooth, satisfying texture rich with fiber, protein, and iron. The decadent orange hue adds a festive and vibrant color to your spread. It's a perfect soup to indulge, especially with the addition of my optional superfoods.

serves: 2

prep: 5 cook: 25 total: 30

egg-free | nut-free | vegan option: omit chicken stock and use vegetable broth

Ingredients
2 tablespoons olive oil

1 medium yellow onion, diced

2 garlic cloves, minced

1 can coconut milk, full fat (do not shake can)

1 cup red lentils

1 (28-oz) can roasted tomatoes

½ teaspoon coriander, ground

pinch of sea salt and black pepper

4 cups vegetable or chicken stock

Method
In a large pot over medium heat add olive oil, onion, and garlic, and sauté until translucent. Without shaking, open the can of coconut milk, and scrape as much fat as you can from the top of the can and add to the onion-garlic mixture, saving the rest of the coconut milk for later. Let simmer for 7 minutes. Add lentils, roasted tomatoes, spices, remaining liquid from coconut can, and let cook for 5 minutes. Lastly, add stock, cover, and let cook for additional 20 minutes, until all ingredients meld together and soften. Remove from heat and pour into a high-speed blender. Blend on high and serve warm.

Optional Superfoods
Per Serving

2 teaspoons pumpkin seeds

2 pinches cayenne pepper

coconut oil (in recipe)

Full-Filling Butternut Squash Soup

serves: 4
prep: 5 cook: 25 total: 30
egg-free | nut-free | dairy-free | vegan option: replace chicken broth with vegetable broth

Ingredients
2 tablespoons olive oil
1 large onion, chopped
5–10 fresh thyme sprigs
4–4 ½ cups butternut
squash, chopped
8-oz can low sodium
garbanzo beans
½ teaspoon salt
½ teaspoon black pepper
¾ teaspoon cumin
4–5 cups vegetable or
chicken stock

Method
In a large saucepan add olive oil, onion, and thyme, and cook for about 5 minutes or until browned. Add remaining ingredients and cook for 20–25 minutes. Once the vegetables are soft, remove thyme sprigs and de-leaf them. Pour soup into a blender and blend until desired consistency. Serve warm in a bowl with fresh thyme garnish on top.

Optional Superfoods
Per Serving
1 teaspoon pumpkin seeds
1 teaspoon harissa
1 teaspoon grated turmeric

Can't Beet This Probiotic Soup

serves: 3
prep: 7 cook: 22 total: 29
egg-free | nut-free option: omit cashews

Ingredients
2 tablespoons olive oil
1 large onion, chopped
5 garlic cloves
2 large cooked beets, cubed
1 teaspoon fennel seeds
1½ cups vegetable or
chicken broth
pinch of salt and pepper
¾ cup low-fat kefir (+ more
for garnish)

Method
Heat olive oil in a large pot over medium heat. Cook onion and garlic for 5 minutes. Add beets and cook another 5 minutes. Add rest of ingredients (except kefir) and continue to cook for another 7 minutes. Remove from heat and let cool for 5 minutes. Pour into high-speed blender and blend on high until all ingredients are mixed together. Return blended soup to the pan and stir in kefir. Serve in bowls with extra fennel seeds on top and a swirl of kefir.

Optional Superfoods
Per Serving

1 teaspoon
popped
amaranth
4 teaspoons
chopped
cashews
½ avocado

Heart and Soul Soup

This soup is so homey to me. I love making it for Kayla, my daughter. It's perfect for those chilly winter days as it warms your heart and soul. A key ingredient to this soup is the farro. Farro is an ancient grain that is from the Mediterranean and contains more fiber than quinoa and is chock-full of wholesomeness. You'll definitely stay cozy with this soup!

serves: 4–6
prep: 5 cook: 25 total: 30
egg-free | nut-free

Ingredients

2 tablespoons olive oil
1 large yellow onion, chopped
2 cups chopped celery
2 cups sliced carrots
3 garlic cloves, minced
2 tablespoons grated fresh ginger
8 cups chicken broth
1½ pounds boneless, skinless chicken breasts, chopped
¾ cup farro
1 tablespoon grated raw turmeric +1 teaspoon ground turmeric
1 teaspoon sea salt
1 teaspoon black pepper

Method

Set a large pot over medium heat. Add the olive oil, chopped onion, celery, carrots, ginger, and garlic. Sauté for 5 minutes to soften. Add the chicken broth, farro, chopped chicken breasts, raw turmeric, ground turmeric, sea salt, and black pepper. Bring to a boil, lower the heat, and simmer for 20–25 minutes. Adjust seasoning to taste. If you prefer stew-based consistency add less chicken broth, or if you prefer more liquid consistency add more chicken broth.

Included Superfoods

Per Serving

ginger
garlic
turmeric

Spiraled Out Salad

If you're looking to have a day with the kids in the kitchen, this is an ideal recipe. Making vegetable "noodles" with a spiralizer is not only fun, but also is a fantastic way to incorporate vegetables into a meal without making them look like traditional veggies. I added apple cider vinegar with the mother to the dressing because of its superb goodness. The key to this vinegar is the "mother," which is a culture of the beneficial bacteria that makes regular apple cider vinegar (also known as ACV) into a murky, cloudy, liquid. So go ahead and make eating vegetables fun for your kids!

---

serves: 4

prep: 20 cook: 5 total: 25

egg-free | dairy-free | nut-free option: omit almonds

Ingredients
2 medium-sized tuna steaks

4 cups mixed greens

2 cups carrot "noodles" made with a spiralizer

2 cups cucumber "noodles" made with a spiralizer

3 tablespoons white and black sesame seeds, toasted

1 (15.5-oz) can low sodium white beans

1 avocado, quartered

Dressing
3 tablespoons apple cider vinegar

1 teaspoon finely minced fresh ginger

1 clove minced garlic

2 tablespoons coconut nectar

¼ cup sesame oil

pinch of sea salt and black pepper

Method
Sear tuna steaks for 1 minute on each side on medium heat or until desired doneness is reached. Once done remove from heat, cool, and slice. Set aside.

For the Salad
In a large bowl combine greens, carrots, cucumbers, sesame seeds, and beans. Set aside.

For the Dressing
In a small bowl whisk together apple cider vinegar, minced garlic, ginger, coconut nectar, sesame oil, pinch of sea salt, and black pepper.

Once all steps are completed, toss the salad with the dressing and arrange on a plate. Top with seared tuna and avocado.

Optional Superfoods
Per Serving

½ clove black garlic

1 tablespoon toasted almonds

1 tablespoon hemp seeds

Festive Quinoa Chicken Salad

This salad reminds me of the holidays but it is great year-round. It is not only appealing to the eyes because of all the beautiful colors but also appealing to your tummy. My addition of dried cranberries gives you the same nutrients as fresh cranberries do. Toss this salad in a matter of no time and bring it to your next festivity.

serves: 4

prep: 10 cook: 10 total: 20

dairy-free | egg-free | nut-free option: omit nuts

Ingredients
2 tablespoons olive oil
½ cup onion, finely chopped
2 cups butternut squash, chopped
pinch of sea salt and black pepper
2 cups cooked white quinoa
12 ounces cooked chicken breast, boneless and skinless
⅓ cup dried cranberries
3 tablespoons toasted walnuts

Quick Balsamic Vinaigrette Dressing
½ cup avocado oil (or olive oil)
¼ cup balsamic vinegar
1 teaspoon pure maple syrup
1 teaspoon Dijon mustard
1 garlic clove, minced
pinch of sea salt and black pepper

Method
Heat a pan on a medium heat and add 2 tablespoons olive oil. Add the chopped onion and butternut squash, sea salt, and pepper, and sauté for 10 minutes. While the onion-butternut squash mixture is cooking, in a large salad bowl add cooked quinoa, chicken, cranberries, and toasted walnuts. Once the onion-butternut squash is finished, add to bowl and dress with the balsamic vinaigrette dressing.

For Quick Balsamic Vinaigrette Dressing
Whisk all the ingredients in a small bowl until combined.

Optional Superfoods
Per Serving

¼ teaspoon sesame seeds
1 pinch cayenne pepper
¼ avocado

Goddess Salad

How does a goddess do everything and keep that fabulous figure? With this goddess salad, of course! On top of it being effortless and delicious, the kalamata olives are abundant in monounsaturated fats, which are good for the heart. They lower levels of bad cholesterol while raising levels of good cholesterol. Put your goddess shoes on and get ready to feel lean and mean after having this salad.

serves: 4

prep: 15 cook: 0 total: 15

egg-free | nut-free | dairy-free option: omit feta

Ingredients
12 oz boneless skinless cooked chicken breast, sliced
4 cups romaine lettuce leaves, chopped
3 Persian (mini) cucumbers, diced
3 medium Roma tomatoes, diced
1 small red onion, sliced
⅓ cup pitted kalamata olives
1 medium red pepper, sliced and deseeded
½ cup low fat feta cheese
½ teaspoon each salt and black pepper
4 tablespoons olive oil
Juice of 1 lemon
2 100% whole wheat pita bread, toasted (each cut in half)

Method
Combine all ingredients except the whole wheat pita and mix together in a large bowl. Next, arrange ingredients on plates in equal portions. Serve with whole wheat pita bread on the side.

Optional Superfoods
Per Serving

1 tablespoon chia seeds
1 tablespoon sunflower seeds
4 handfuls of broccoli sprouts

Cleansing Tabbouleh Salad

Think of this recipe as tabbouleh salad on steroids. It is a daily nourishment in the Mediterranean. Back home we had it in the morning, afternoon, and at night. If you haven't heard of cauliflower rice yet, get ready! Besides being easy and quick to cook, it simulates the texture of couscous, is light and fluffy, and is nutritive. Not convinced? It helps with blood pressure, kidney function, and boosts brain health—enough said. After you consume this salad, blast "Eye of the Tiger" and you'll be ready to conquer the world!

serves: 4
prep: 15 cook: 0 total: 15
egg-free | dairy-free | nut-free | vegan

Ingredients

Salad
2 cups cooked quinoa
1½ cups of cauliflower "rice" (add chopped cauliflower to high-speed blender to make "rice")
2 cups cherry tomatoes, sliced
2 cups fresh parsley, minced
1 cup finely chopped celery
¾ cup cilantro, minced
4 green onions, sliced
¼ cup chopped mint
1 whole avocado (quartered)

Dressing
3 tablespoons olive oil
½ teaspoon sea salt
½ teaspoon black pepper
juice from 1 lemon
1 clove garlic, minced

Method
Mix all salad ingredients (except avocado) in a bowl and set aside.

In a small bowl combine all ingredients for dressing and whisk together. Then add the dressing to the salad and combine. Top with avocado.

Sima's Tip
I'm seriously obsessed with this salad! Sometimes I drizzle raw tahini on top, or red pepper flakes and add it to any of the egg dishes. Yum! To keep fresh, store in an airtight container in the refrigerator for up to 2 days.

Optional Superfoods
Per Serving

garlic (in recipe)
1 tablespoon hemp seed
pinch of red pepper flakes

Taco Salad on the Go

This is the perfect solution for busy people on the go and who want a healthy alternative to tacos. I prepare it the night before and store it in reCAP Mason Jars, which is my absolute favorite brand. In a jar, it looks just like a meal you picked up from a health food store—it's okay, I promise I won't tell.

serves: 4
prep: 15 cook: 15 total: 30
egg-free | nut-free | dairy-free option: replace yogurt with nondairy yogurt

Ingredients
2 tablespoons olive oil
1 lb. lean ground turkey
1 (15.5-oz) can low sodium black beans, drained
3 tablespoons taco seasoning (see recipe below)
4 cups (about 1 head) romaine lettuce, chopped into small pieces
3 medium tomatoes, chopped
1 medium red onion, chopped
1 whole fresh jalapeño, chopped (remove seeds if you don't like it spicy)
8 tablespoons 2% Greek yogurt, plain juice from 1 lemon

Garnish (optional)
1 cup chopped cilantro

Taco Seasoning Mix
1 tablespoon chili powder
½ teaspoon garlic powder
½ teaspoon onion powder
¼ teaspoon red pepper flakes
½ teaspoon oregano
1½ teaspoons sweet paprika
½ tablespoon cumin
1½ teaspoons sea salt
2 teaspoons black pepper

Method
In a large skillet over medium high heat, add olive oil and ground turkey and cook for about 10–12 minutes or until cooked thoroughly. Add black beans, taco seasoning mix, and set aside to cool. Then, take 4 mason jars and layer equal amounts of lettuce, chopped tomatoes, turkey-black bean mixture, red onion, and jalapeño. Top with 2 tablespoons of Greek yogurt in each, cilantro (if using), lemon juice, and more taco seasoning mix. Once all ingredients have been added, close the jars and store in refrigerator until ready to grab and go. When ready to eat, shake vigorously to combine. Will stay fresh in the refrigerator for 1–2 days.

For Taco Seasoning Mix
Mix all spices in an airtight container and store in a cool place.

Optional Superfoods
Per Serving

1 tablespoon ground flaxseeds
4 handfuls of sprouts
red pepper flakes (included in recipe)

Party It Up Salad

When I get invited to parties, this is my go-to party dish. It's nourishing, appetizing, and easy to make. The best part of this salad is that you can swap ingredients in and out depending on the season. Make a double batch and watch this salad disappear quickly.

serves: 4
prep: 15 cook: 0 total: 15
egg-free | dairy-free option: omit feta | nut-free option: omit nuts

Ingredients
1 cup cooked quinoa
16 oz pre-cooked baby
   beets, chopped
4 cups spinach, chopped
1 cup fresh blueberries
½ cup red grapes,
   halved
⅓ cup low fat feta
   cheese, crumbled
¼ cup raw walnuts,
   chopped
½ cup pomegranate
   arils

Pomegranate Lemon Dressing
¼ cup lemon juice
1½ tablespoons
   pomegranate
   molasses
2 tablespoons olive oil
1 garlic clove, minced
½ teaspoon sea salt
½ teaspoon black
   pepper

Method
In a large bowl, mix all of the ingredients together except pomegranate arils. Then, in a lidded container mix all dressing ingredients and shake vigorously until combined. Add dressing to salad, coat thoroughly, and top with pomegranate arils and serve.

Included Superfoods
Per Serving

garlic
pomegranate
1 teaspoon flaxseeds

Stuffed Sweet Potato with Warm Bean Salad

Here we go with another delicious recipe containing, you guessed it: my favorite, sweet potatoes. Imagine the beautiful orange-colored sweet potato filled with protein-rich cannellini beans and gorgeous red tomatoes, spiced up and drizzled with raw tahini. YUM!

---

serves: 2

prep: 10 cook: 12 total: 22

egg-free | nut-free | dairy-free | vegan

Ingredients
2 medium sweet potatoes

Bean Salad
1 tablespoon olive oil
½ medium red onion, chopped
1 garlic clove, minced
1 medium red bell pepper, diced
1 (15-oz) can no salt added cannellini beans, drained and rinsed
1 cup cherry tomatoes, halved
juice of 1 lemon
pinch of sea salt and black pepper
2 tablespoons raw tahini

Method
Prick sweet potatoes all over with a fork and microwave for 6–8 minutes. Set aside. Heat 1 tablespoon of olive oil in a small saucepan over medium heat. Add chopped red onion and garlic, and sauté for 2 minutes. Add the bell pepper and cook for another 2 minutes. Add the beans and tomatoes and cook for 2 additional minutes. Remove from heat and add lemon juice, salt, and pepper. Next, when potatoes are cool, make a small cut lengthwise and press open to make a well in the center. Spoon the bean-bell pepper salad into the 2 potatoes, in equal amounts. Drizzle each half with 1 tablespoon of raw tahini.

Optional Superfoods
Per Serving

1 pinch of cayenne
garlic (included in recipe)
tahini (included in recipe)

Sunset

This section of *Sima's Healthy Indulgence* includes recipes for dinner dishes that will leave you satisfied. I guarantee that these dishes will take you back in time before Instagramming, tweeting, or snapping your food was even relevant. These dishes are so appealing to the eyes and stomach that you'll devour the whole thing right away and forget to post to your social media.

There are two factors to keep in mind regarding dinner. First, eating three hours before bedtime is recommended because this gives your body time to properly digest food at night. The earlier you eat and sleep, the better it is for your mind-body balance and overall peak functioning for the next day. The second factor is no carbs at night, only protein paired with vegetables and a small amount of friendly fats (a.k.a. PVF combo for dinner). With that being said, grab your cooking apron and let's get to cooking dinner.

SUNSET RECIPES

Speedy Shawarma

Shawarma is meat that has been slowly roasting on a spit all day, dripping with juices and flavor, waiting to be carved to order. But let's face reality—unfortunately, we don't have all day to be roasting meat. So, I've come up with a speedy version for you to get that perfect and full flavor in just 30 minutes! Pair this delicious recipe with a side of Israeli chopped salad, and you got yourself the perfect supper.

serves: 4
prep: 10 cook: 20 total: 30
egg-free | nut-free | dairy-free

Ingredients
2 boneless skinless chicken breasts
2 tablespoons olive oil
1 tablespoon shawarma spice mix
  (recipe below)
1 large onion, chopped
1 garlic clove, minced
1 tablespoon lemon juice
¼ teaspoon each sea salt and black pepper

Shawarma Spice:
1 teaspoon each ground allspice,
  cinnamon, cumin, ginger, turmeric,
  and black pepper

Tahini Sauce
½ cup tahini
1 cup water
1 small garlic clove, minced
1 tablespoon lemon juice
pinch of sea salt

Israeli Chopped Salad:
4 small plum tomatoes
2 Persian cucumber, chopped
½ medium onion, chopped
3 small radishes, grated
3 tablespoons olive oil
juice of 1 lemon
¼ teaspoon sea salt
¼ teaspoon black pepper

Method
Cut the chicken into thin, long strips, season with 1 tablespoon olive oil and shawarma spice, and set aside. Lightly coat a skillet with 1 tablespoon olive oil and sauté onion until browned. Add garlic to skillet along with chicken strips and cook chicken through for about 10–12 minutes. Drizzle with lemon juice. Serve with Israeli salad and tahini sauce.

For the Shawarma Spice
Mix all ingredients in an airtight container or mason jar.

For the Tahini Sauce
In a small bowl, combine tahini and water and mix well to make a paste. Add garlic, lemon juice, and sea salt. Mix thoroughly.

For the Israeli Chopped Salad
In a medium bowl mix tomatoes, cucumber, onion, and radishes. In a separate bowl whisk together the remaining ingredients. Combine and enjoy.

Optional Superfoods
Per Serving

1 clove black garlic (for tahini)
½ tablespoon harissa
¼ teaspoon red chili flakes

Day at the Spa

Looking for something light and refreshing just like a day at the spa? This Thai salad has only 8 ingredients and is pure bliss. Colorful and refreshing on the tongue, you'll definitely want to make this salad again and again whenever you want to feel euphoric.

serves: 4
prep: 15 cook: 0 total: 15
egg-free | dairy-free | nut-free option: omit almonds

Ingredients

4 cups Napa cabbage, thinly sliced
2 cups red cabbage, thinly sliced
2 medium carrots, grated
4 green onions, thinly sliced
2 tablespoons raw turmeric, grated
½ cup cilantro, chopped (plus extra for garnish)
12 oz cooked boneless, skinless chicken breast
3 tablespoons toasted almonds

Dressing

juice of 1 lime
3 teaspoons coconut nectar
2 teaspoons minced garlic
2 teaspoons minced ginger
1 teaspoon red pepper flakes (optional)

Method

In a large serving bowl, combine all salad ingredients and mix with dressing until thoroughly coated. Serve in bowls and garnish with chopped cilantro.

For the Dressing

In a lidded container or mason jar combine lime juice, coconut nectar, garlic, ginger, and red pepper flakes. Shake vigorously.

Optional Superfoods

Per Serving

1 tablespoon hemp seeds
raw turmeric (included in recipe)
garlic (included in recipe)

Holy Guacamole Fajitas

My version of fajitas will make you say, "Amen!" once you are finished eating! Fajitas comes from the Spanish word "faja," meaning skirt, because it is originally made with skirt steak. But the secret to making this Healthy Indulgence-approved dish is using chicken with plenty of vegetables. The aroma of the spices with the mixture of onions and peppers is absolutely intoxicating and will have you saying your thanks and prayers.

serves: 4
prep: 12 cook: 18 total: 30
egg-free | dairy-free | nut-free

Ingredients
Chicken Fajitas
2 teaspoons extra-virgin olive oil
1 medium red onion, thinly sliced
2 red bell peppers, thinly sliced
2 orange bell peppers, thinly sliced
1 jalapeño, thinly sliced and de-seeded
16 oz cooked chicken, sliced thinly
4 tablespoons cilantro, chopped
1 lime, quartered

Fajita Seasoning Mix
¼ cup chili powder
2 tablespoons paprika (sweet or spicy)
1 tablespoon onion powder
1 tablespoon garlic powder
1½ tablespoons sea salt
1 tablespoon cumin powder

Guacamole
1 whole avocado
¼ red onion, finely chopped
juice of 1 lime
½ teaspoon sea salt

Method
Coat a cast-iron skillet with the olive oil. Once heated through add the onion, bell peppers, and jalapeño and cook through for about 5 minutes or until soft. Once the mixture browns, coat with 2–3 teaspoons of fajita seasoning and add chicken. Cook and stir mixture for 10 more minutes and turn off heat. Finish with a squeeze of a lime, garnish with chopped cilantro, and serve with guacamole.

For the Fajita Seasoning Mix
Mix all spices in an airtight container and store in a cool place.

For the Guacamole
Cut avocado in half and remove pit. Scrape out avocado, place in a bowl, and use a fork to mash until it becomes smooth. Lastly, add sea salt, red onion, and lime juice and thoroughly mix together. Serve immediately.

Optional Superfoods
Per Serving

¼ teaspoon popped amaranth (for guacamole)
½ tablespoon harissa
¼ teaspoon cayenne (for fajitas)

Powered Up Steak

Who doesn't love a juicy steak? It is one of the best protein-packed meats you can consume. It contains iron, B vitamins, and a host of other minerals that just cannot be found in any other protein. Pair your steak with a bed of spinach, and you'll feel powered up!

---

serves: 4

prep: 10 cook: 10 total: 20

egg-free | nut-free | dairy-free

Ingredients

Steak
1 tablespoon olive oil
1½ lb. skirt steak
1 tablespoon sea salt
1 teaspoon ground black
   pepper
1 bunch spinach
2 medium tomatoes, chopped
2 tablespoons toasted
   pumpkin seeds

Cilantro Dressing
½ cup extra-virgin olive oil
¼ cup lime juice
½ cup packed fresh cilantro,
   chopped
½ teaspoon sea salt
2 tablespoons fresh orange
   juice
½ tablespoon coconut nectar
1 clove whole garlic

Method
Add all dressing ingredients to a high-speed blender and blend on high. Then, in a grill pan add olive oil and heat thoroughly. Add steak and grill for 5 minutes, seasoning with salt and pepper. Flip steak over, add some more salt and pepper, and cook for another 3–5 minutes, depending on the desired doneness. Lastly, on a large platter place your spinach and chopped tomatoes and layer with the sliced steak. Sprinkle with pumpkin seeds and drizzle with the cilantro dressing; serve warm.

Optional Superfoods
Per Serving

1 teaspoon whole
   flaxseeds
garlic (in recipe)
pumpkin seeds (in
   recipe)

Ahi-lievable Fennel and Apple

If you need to whip up a simple but unbelievable meal to impress your guests, this is the dish to make. Fennel is an eco-friendly plant as you can use the bulb, seeds, and leaves. Pair this fennel salad with ahi and apples and you'll have your guests saying it was ahi-mazing!

serves: 4
prep: 10 cook: 10 total: 20
egg-free | nut-free | dairy-free

Ingredients
4 tablespoons olive oil +1 teaspoon
1 large garlic clove, finely chopped
4 (5-oz) Ahi tuna fillets
1 teaspoon sea salt
1 teaspoon ground black pepper

Fennel and Apple Salad
2 fennel bulbs, trimmed, halved, cored and thinly sliced on a mandolin
2 medium apples, halved, cored, and sliced
2 celery stalks, sliced diagonally
¾ cup walnuts, chopped and toasted

Dressing
1 teaspoon Dijon mustard
2 tablespoons apple cider vinegar (with the "mother")
3 tablespoons extra-virgin olive oil
2 tablespoons fresh lemon juice
½ teaspoon sea salt
½ teaspoon black pepper

Method
In a skillet, add 1 teaspoon olive oil and sauté the garlic over medium heat. Season ahi with sea salt and black pepper and place in skillet. Sear for about 4 minutes on each side or until fish has firmed up (cook longer for less pink in the center). For best results when cooking ahi, add 1 teaspoon of olive oil to skillet and cook 1 fillet at a time. Repeat process with each fillet. Remove from skillet and serve with salad.

For the Salad
In a large bowl whisk together all ingredients for dressing. Once mixed, add fennel, apples, celery, and chopped walnuts. Toss salad.

Optional Superfoods
Per Serving

1 tablespoon black sesame seeds
1 tablespoon toasted pumpkin seeds
¼ avocado

Zoodle My Noodle

I know, I know, zoodles don't compare to regular pasta. But let me convince you that these "noodles" are much better for you than pasta and are even fun to make! This rustic dish that's been given a modern twist will bring an aromatic flavor of herbes de Provence to your turkey meat that will whisk you away to the countryside. Zoodle away!

serves: 4
prep: 10 cook: 12 total: 22
egg-free | dairy-free | nut-free option: omit walnuts and pine nuts

Ingredients
4 zucchinis
1 medium onion
3 tablespoons extra-
    virgin olive oil
2 garlic cloves,
    minced
1 pound lean ground
    turkey
1 tablespoon herbes
    de Provence
½ teaspoon each
    sea salt and black
    pepper

Method
Spiralize your zucchinis into long "noodle" strands and set aside. Next, finely dice the onion and add into a pan along with 1 tablespoon of olive oil. Cook onion through until browned, add in minced garlic, and sauté, making sure garlic doesn't burn. Add the remaining 2 tablespoons olive oil, ground turkey, sea salt, black pepper, and herbes de Provence to the pan and cook thoroughly. Place noodles in a bowl, add the ground turkey, and mix altogether. Serve and zoodle away!

Optional Superfoods
Per Serving

1 tablespoon
    coconut oil
1 tablespoon
    pine nuts
1 clove black
    garlic

Chimichurri Olé

Tango, gauchos, and beef come to mind when I think of chimichurri. Chimichurri is a famous sauce in Argentina and in this recipe, I add it to my steak lettuce cups, which gives it a flash of flavor and a kick of spiciness. Olé!

serves: 4
prep: 15 cook: 10 total: 25
egg-free | nut-free | dairy-free

Ingredients

Chimichurri Sauce
1 cup Italian flat-leaf parsley
1 tablespoon freshly minced
    garlic
⅛ cup fresh oregano
2½ tablespoons red wine
    vinegar
¼ teaspoon red pepper flakes
¼ teaspoon sea salt
¼ teaspoon black pepper
½ cup olive oil

Steak
1½ lbs skirt steak
½ teaspoon sea salt, divided
½ teaspoon black pepper
2 tablespoons olive oil
Butter lettuce leaves, about 2–3
    leaves per person

Method

In a high-speed blender or food processor blend all the chimichurri sauce ingredients except for the oil; while blending, pour in olive oil slowly. Next, season the steak with salt and pepper. Heat a skillet over medium heat, add 2 tablespoons of olive oil, and then add the meat to the pan. Cook for 3–5 minutes on each side or until desired doneness is achieved.

Once cooled, cut meat, place in a lettuce leaf and wrap. Top off with 2 tablespoons of chimichurri sauce per wrap.

Sima's Tip

I love parsley! Parsley is loaded with so many health benefits, from boosting the immune system to aiding with water retention and indigestion.

Optional Superfoods
Per Serving

chili flakes (included
    in recipe)
garlic (included in
    recipe)
1 teaspoon harissa
    sauce

Kick Some Ass-Paragus!

Sometimes less is more. For this recipe, your two star ingredients are eggs and asparagus. Asparagus is a vegetable known for its ability to neutralize cell-damaging free radicals and it naturally detoxifies the body. It's also a great way to keep your kidneys functioning properly because of the high levels of fiber and potassium. Use these two ingredients to replenish your body after a long day!

---

serves: 2
prep: 5 cook: 10 total: 15
dairy-free | nut-free

Ingredients
2 tablespoons coconut oil
12 spears of asparagus, ends cut off
2 teaspoons lemon juice
4 eggs
½ teaspoon black pepper
½ teaspoon sea salt

Method
In a skillet over medium heat, add 1 tablespoon of coconut oil and sauté your asparagus for 5 minutes until softened. Drizzle with lemon juice and set aside. In the same skillet, add remaining 1 tablespoon of coconut oil and cook your eggs sunny side up for 3–4 minutes until yolks have set up but are still runny. Serve asparagus on plate, top with 2 eggs per person, and season with sea salt and pepper.

Sima's Tip
Did you know that asparagus is great for your sex life? For centuries, it has been famous for its powerful aphrodisiac qualities.

Optional Superfoods
Per Serving

coconut oil (included in recipe)
1 teaspoon hemp seeds
¼ teaspoon cayenne pepper

Spiced Up Ahi

This Asian-influenced dish is simple, elegant, and Healthy Indulgence-approved. It is a lean and clean recipe that is brimming with flavor and spice. It contains sesame seeds, which are packed with calcium and properties that will elevate your mood.

serves: 4
prep: 15 cook: 15 total: 30
egg-free | nut-free | dairy-free

Ingredients

Wasabi Marinade
1 tablespoon wasabi paste
1 tablespoon dry mustard seed, ground
⅓ cup Japanese sake (optional)
⅓ cup rice wine vinegar
1 tablespoon fresh ginger, grated
½ teaspoon white sesame seeds, toasted

Tuna
4 (5-oz) tuna steaks
2 tablespoons sesame oil
1 teaspoon minced garlic
4 cups broccoli florets, chopped
¼ teaspoon sea salt
¼ teaspoon black pepper

Method

For Wasabi Marinade
Mix all ingredients together in a bowl until thoroughly dissolved. Once ready, place in a lidded container with tuna and marinate for 10 minutes.

For Tuna
After tuna has marinated, place a skillet over medium heat and add 1 tablespoon of sesame oil. Season fillets with salt and pepper, place into a pan, and cook for 4–5 minutes on each side. Once fully cooked, set aside.

In another skillet over low heat, add remaining 1 tablespoon of sesame oil and add minced garlic. Add chopped broccoli and sauté for 3–5 minutes. Remove from heat and serve with tuna.

Optional Superfoods
Per Serving

garlic (included in recipe)
sesame seeds (included in recipe)
sesame oil (included in recipe)

Kabob-in Greece

This authentic Mediterranean kabob is grilled to perfection, and the addition of a gorgeous Greek salad makes it even more delectable. It's bursting with flavor and freshness that will leave you satisfied.

---

makes: 8–10 small kabobs or 4–6 large kabobs
prep: 10 cook: 15 total: 25
dairy-free | egg-free | nut-free

Ingredients

Kabob
1½ lbs lean ground beef
1 large onion, finely chopped
¼ cup parsley, finely chopped
¼ cup mint, finely chopped
1 large egg
2 teaspoons ground cumin
1 tablespoon paprika
1 teaspoon black pepper
2 tablespoons tomato paste
juice of ½ lemon
Wooden skewers

Salad
½ cup low fat feta cheese, crumbled
4 cups romaine lettuce leaves, chopped
1 large cucumber, diced
5 Roma tomatoes, diced
1 red onion, sliced
⅓ cup pitted kalamata olives
1 bell pepper, sliced and deseeded
½ teaspoon each sea salt and black pepper
1 lemon, quartered

Method
Mix all ingredients in a bowl (do not overmix because the meat will harden if overmixed) except skewers. Form meat mixture into balls and place onto wooden skewers. Place on a grill pan to cook on each side for 10–12 minutes, until desired doneness.

For the Salad
Mix all salad ingredients together in a bowl. Arrange on plates in equal portions and finish with a squeeze of a lemon. Serve with kabobs on the side.

Optional Superfoods
Per Serving

1 tablespoon chia seeds
1 tablespoon sunflower seeds
handful of broccoli sprouts

Just like the name of this dish, this frittata is good anytime of the day. I've made it with cauliflower "rice," which is just grating or pulsing a whole head of cauliflower in a food processor. This dish is low carb and low lactose, making it completely revamped and good for your body.

serves: 4–6
prep: 5 cook: 25 total: 30

Ingredients

1 tablespoon coconut oil
1 cup cauliflower "rice"
1 cup kale, shredded
5 large egg whites
3 large eggs
2 tablespoons unsweetened almond milk
½ teaspoon fresh rosemary, chopped
¼ teaspoon garlic powder
½ teaspoon sea salt and black pepper
5 oz goat cheese

Method

Preheat oven to 375°. Heat iron skillet over medium heat and add coconut oil. Add "rice" cauliflower and cook for 3–5 minutes or until soft. Add kale and cook until semi wilted. Next, in a bowl whisk all remaining ingredients except the goat cheese. Add egg mixture to the skillet and let cook for a few minutes. Remove from heat and place in oven for 20 minutes until edges are set. Remove from oven, garnish with goat cheese, and let cool for 5 minutes. Serve warm.

Optional Superfoods

Per Serving

kale (included in recipe)
½ teaspoon turmeric powder
1 black garlic clove (mix in goat cheese)

Guilt-Free Turkey and Mash

Sometimes you just need the comforting feeling of home and holidays. This recipe can be made in just 20 minutes and still taste like you've been cooking all day. The cauliflower mash is a great substitute to carb-filled mashed potatoes, making this a "holiday meal" you can eat without the guilt.

---

serves: 4
prep: 5 cook: 25 total: 30
egg-free | *dairy-free* | *nut-free*

Ingredients
1 package of pre-cooked roasted
  turkey breast, sliced
  (not deli meat); 1 slice per person

Cauliflower Mash
1 large sized head of cauliflower,
  chopped into florets
3 roasted garlic cloves
pinch of sea salt and black pepper
2 tablespoons vegan butter (such
  as Earth Balance)
2 teaspoons fresh thyme leaves
1 teaspoon chives, chopped

Method
Fill a large pot with water and bring to a boil. Add cauliflower florets. Once boiling, reduce heat to a simmer and cover. Allow cauliflower to boil for about 6–8 minutes or until tender. Drain the steamed cauliflower (save 3 tablespoons of the water for later use) and transfer to a high-speed blender. Add in roasted garlic, sea salt, black pepper, saved 3 tablespoons of water, and butter. Process on high until it becomes the consistency of a mash. Serve with turkey breast and garnish with thyme and chives.

Optional Superfoods
Per Serving

1 teaspoon hemp
  seeds
¼ teaspoon turmeric
  powder
garlic (included in
  recipe)

Anti-Aging Shakshuka

This green shakshuka is cousins with my Jerusalem shakshuka (page 65). The secret to this shakshuka are the greens in it, specifically the beet greens. Beet greens contain fiber, vitamins, and best of all is that they are considered to be anti-aging and good for the skin. So ladies and gentlemen, listen up, toss the anti-aging creams away, and load up on this dish!

---

serves: 2
prep: 7 cook: 13 total: 20
dairy-free | nut-free option: omit walnuts

Ingredients
2 teaspoons extra-virgin olive oil
1 onion, chopped
2 garlic cloves, chopped
½ fresh jalapeño, seeded and chopped (more if you like it spicy)
½ teaspoon ground cumin
6 cups mixed greens (i.e. beet greens, spinach, or kale)
4 eggs
½ teaspoon sea salt
½ teaspoon black pepper

Method
In a hot pan add 2 teaspoons of olive oil. Sauté onion, garlic, jalapeño, and cumin for 5 minutes or until browned. Add your choice of mixed greens and cook for another 3 minutes. Once your greens are cooked, crack eggs on top (make sure eggs are spaced out around pan) and cook for additional 5 minutes. Top with black pepper and sea salt.

Optional Superfoods
Per Serving

½ teaspoon chili flakes
½ teaspoon powdered turmeric
1 tablespoon walnuts

Perfect Niçoise

I love salads for dinner because they are customizable, easy to put together, and yet still so nutritional! This is my version of the classic salade niçoise and it contains ingredients that help lower cholesterol and are a great source of magnesium and folate.

serves: 4
prep: 10 cook: 10 total: 20
dairy-free | nut-free

Ingredients

Dressing
½ cup extra-virgin olive oil
juice of 1 large lemon
1 tablespoon mustard
1 tablespoon yellow mustard seeds
pinch of sea salt and black pepper

Salad
1 small head of crisp lettuce,
    rinsed, dried, and chopped (any
    kind)
3 tablespoons fresh basil, chopped
2 cups green beans, steamed
1 cup chopped asparagus, steamed
2 cans albacore tuna in olive oil
2 tablespoons capers
1 Persian cucumber, thinly sliced
2 medium carrots, chopped
1 cup red cherry tomatoes, halved
6 radishes, sliced
4 hard-boiled eggs, halved
1 red bell pepper, cut into rounds
½ cup black olives

Method

For the Dressing
Whisk together all the dressing
    ingredients and set aside.

For the Salad
First, put the lettuce in a large
bowl or platter and arrange the
basil over the lettuce. Second,
put the green beans and
asparagus in the middle of the
salad. Third, add the tuna and
top tuna with capers. Fourth,
arrange the cucumber slices
and carrots next to the beans.
Fifth, scatter the tomatoes,
radishes, eggs, peppers, and
olives all around. Lastly, drizzle
the dressing all over and toss
ingredients together.

Optional Superfoods
Per Serving

1 tablespoon black
    sesame seeds
1 tablespoon
    sunflower seeds
1 tablespoon
    pomegranate arils

Maple Salmon

This maple roasted salmon recipe is delicious, but with a side of Brussels sprouts it is to die for! Brussels sprouts are high in protein for a green vegetable and just one serving meets your vitamin C and K intake for the day. The way that the Brussels are roasted brings out a sweet, nutty flavor that complements the maple flavor of the fish.

serves: 4
prep: 10 cook: 20 total: 30
egg-free | nut-free | dairy-free

Ingredients
1 lb Brussels sprouts, trimmed and halved
2 tablespoons olive oil
1 large onion, cut into wedges
¼ teaspoon each sea salt and black pepper
2 tablespoons pure maple syrup
2 tablespoons Dijon mustard
½ lb skinless salmon fillet, cut into 4 pieces
lemon wedges, for serving

Method
Heat oven to 450°. Mix Brussels sprouts, oil, onion, salt, and pepper and place on a baking sheet in the middle of the oven to cook for 10 minutes. Then in a small bowl, mix together the maple syrup, mustard, and ¼ teaspoon each of salt and pepper. On a second baking sheet, place 4 salmon fillets and pour sauce over them and cook for 8–10 minutes until the salmon has firmed up and browned. Serve the fish with Brussels sprouts and lemon wedges.

Optional Superfoods
Per Serving

1 teaspoon black sesame seeds
1 teaspoon minced garlic (to marinade)
1 clove garlic (to marinade)

Snacks

Most
diets warn and scare you
away from snacking between meals,
claiming it's a taboo. But it's certainly not taboo
here! In fact, I preach and practice just the opposite.
Snacking is an essential part of a healthy and nutritious
diet and a critical component for achieving your weight-loss
goals. The scientific truth is that snacking (the Healthy Indulgence way, of course) speeds up your metabolism, boosts your
energy, heightens your concentration, and stabilizes your blood
sugar, and also will keep unnecessary cravings away. It is important
to remember that you need to snack effectively, which means you
need to eat every 3 hours, so make sure you grab that morning
and night snack in-between your three main meals of breakfast, lunch, and dinner. Happy snacking!

SNACKS RECIPES

Positivity Smoothie

When you blend bananas, almond butter, almond milk, and maca powder, you get a rich and vitamin-filled smoothie with a kick that will energize you for the day ahead. Maca is a superfood rich in vitamins B, C, and E, which help balance your hormones and mood. Drink this smoothie in the morning and all the positivity will come rolling your way!

serves: 1
prep: 5 cook: 0 total: 5
egg-free | dairy-free | nut-free option: replace almond milk
with coconut milk and omit almond butter

Ingredients
1 frozen banana
1 cup unsweetened almond milk
1 tablespoon almond butter
1 heaping tablespoon maca powder
½ teaspoon pure vanilla extract
1 scoop dairy free protein powder

Method
Add all ingredients to a high-speed blender and blend for 2–3 minutes or until smooth and creamy. Pour into a glass and enjoy.

Sima's Tip
If you have a nut allergy, feel free to substitute your favorite seed butter instead. Hemp and sunflower butter are a great options.

Replenish and Restore Smoothie

You've just finished your workout. You're looking to replenish your body and you want to do it fast. Try this quick, refreshing recipe filled with protein, carbs, and antioxidants. Recover and restore!

serves: 1
prep: 5 cook: 0 total: 5
nut-free | dairy-free | vegan

Ingredients
1 cup fresh pineapple (frozen works too)
½ medium banana (fresh or frozen)
½ teaspoon ground turmeric
1 cup coconut water
¼ avocado
3–4 ice cubes
1 scoop dairy free protein powder

Method
Add all ingredients to a high-speed blender and blend for 2–3 minutes or until smooth and creamy. Pour into a glass and enjoy.

Fueled Up Trail Mix

Keep a bag of this trail mix in your purse, backpack, kids' lunch boxes, or your car, and you're ready to fuel up no matter where you are. It's salty, crunchy, and has just enough sweetness from the chocolate chips to satisfy your sweet craving. Feeling energized? Check. Sweet tooth satisfied? Check. Nut free? Check.

---

makes: 10–12 (4 tablespoons per serving)
prep: 5 cook: 15 total: 20
nut-free | dairy-free | egg-free | vegan

Ingredients

Chili-rubbed Roasted Pumpkin Seeds
1 cup raw pumpkin seeds
¼ cup black chia seeds
1 teaspoon chili powder (optional)
1 teaspoon cumin
pinch of sea salt and black pepper
2–3 tablespoons water

Trail Mix
1 cup raw, unsalted sunflower seeds
1 cup chili-rubbed roasted pumpkin seeds
½ cup each mixed dried blueberries and unsweetened dried cherries
¼ cup dairy free chocolate chips

Method

For the Chili-rubbed Roasted Pumpkin Seeds
Preheat oven to 350°. In a small bowl, combine raw pumpkin seeds, chia seeds, chili powder, cumin, salt, and pepper. Add water so mixture is damp, but not soaked. Layer the seed mixture on a baking sheet in an even and thin layer. Bake for 10 minutes. Remove from oven, flip, and then bake for 5 more minutes. Remove from the oven and allow to cool.

For the Trail Mix
In an airtight container, combine all ingredients and store in a cool and dry place.

Cherry Tahini Exercise Bites

These little bites of goodness are amazing not just in flavor, but are also packed with ingredients that will give you that extra push to want to exercise. Just try it, you'll know exactly what I am talking about! You'll be pumping that iron or running that mile effortlessly!

makes: 20 bites (2 bites per person)
prep: 15 cook: 0 total: 15
dairy-free | egg-free | vegan

Ingredients
½ cup mixed walnuts and
   pistachios
½ cup raisins
½ cup dried cherries
⅔ cup tahini
½ cup shredded
   unsweetened coconut

Method
Place all ingredients in a food processor or high-speed blender and blend until broken into small pieces and becomes like a sticky dough. Transfer the "dough" to a large bowl, wet the palm of your hands with water, and form 20 balls. Place the balls in the freezer for 5–10 minutes so they become hard. Store in a sealed container in the freezer for up to 3 weeks.

Sima's Tip
For best taste, try them frozen!

Sharing Is Caring Bites

These kale and quinoa bites travel with me everywhere I go, like my entourage. The fact that they are small, like a mini muffin, makes it so easy to consume and share with your family because after all, sharing is caring.

---

makes: 30 bites (3 bites per person)
prep: 10 cook: 20 total: 30
nut-free | dairy-free option: omit feta cheese

Ingredients
1 cup uncooked quinoa
2 cups water
1 teaspoon olive oil
1 cup kale, chopped
½ medium onion, finely chopped
1 clove garlic, minced
¼ teaspoon dried oregano
5 ounces crumbled low-fat feta cheese
3 medium eggs, beaten
pinch of sea salt and black pepper

Method
Preheat oven to 350°. Mix quinoa and water and cook according to package directions. Set aside. Next, in a medium skillet heat olive oil over medium heat. Sauté onion until brown, then add kale. Sauté until kale is cooked through and then remove from heat. In a large bowl combine quinoa, onion-kale mixture, minced garlic, oregano, feta, beaten eggs, sea salt, and pepper. Spray mini muffin tin with nonstick spray or coconut oil and add quinoa-kale mixture. Bake for 20 minutes. Remove from oven and let cool for 5 minutes.

Sima's Tip
Be creative and add your own favorite greens: spinach, broccoli, or even a mix of chopped parsley and cilantro. To keep fresh, store in refrigerator for up to 3–5 days.

Chocolate Joy Ball

These chocolate-cashew balls will radiate happiness! With cacao bringing in all its powerful benefits such as mood elevators, more calcium than cow's milk, and 40 times the antioxidants of blueberries, it is definitely a game changer. Also, the subtle tropical hint of coconut and the sweetness of dates is the perfect marriage for this happily ever after in a snack. Kick back and snack on these little balls packed with live endorphins. #purejoy

---

makes: 15 balls (2 balls per person)
prep: 15 cook: 0 total: 15
dairy-free | egg-free | vegan

Ingredients
1 cup Medjool dates, pitted
¼ cup cacao nibs
¼ cup raw cashews
¼ cup unsweetened shredded coconut
1 lemon, juiced and zested (+2 extra teaspoons of lemon zest to roll balls in)
2 tablespoons unsalted, raw cashew butter
1 tablespoon ground flaxseeds
½ teaspoon pure vanilla extract
1 tablespoon unsweetened cacao powder
1 pinch of sea salt

Method
Place all the ingredients into a high-speed blender or food processor and blend until all ingredients are mixed together. Once the mixture sticks together and forms a sticky dough, remove and place in a large bowl. Use your hands to roll into 15 balls (mixture may be a bit sticky). Roll half (or all) the balls in lemon zest. Place in the freezer for 12 minutes to harden. Remove from freezer and devour!

Sima's Tip
For a different taste, try them frozen!

Grandma's Sloppy Joe Pita

My grandma is famous for creating this recipe, so I can't take full credit for it. When we would walk into her house, we could always smell the aroma floating in the air, and we knew there was something special waiting for us in the kitchen. I did give it a tweak by adding the pomegranate molasses and Mediterranean sauce, which adds a very unique and tart flavor. Nothing is like Grandma's cooking!

serves: 6 (1 pocket per person)
prep: 5 cook: 25 total: 30
dairy-free | egg-free | nut-free option: omit pine nuts

Ingredients
1 large white onion, roughly chopped
1 pound lean ground beef (go for 80/20 and not extra lean)
2 tablespoons pomegranate molasses
1 tablespoon tomato paste
¼ cup toasted pine nuts
2 tablespoons lemon juice
pinch of sea salt and black pepper
1 tablespoon olive oil, for brushing
3 100% whole wheat pita bread, cut into halves, and toasted

Garnish
½ cup pomegranate arils
½ cup chopped parsley
6 teaspoons pine nuts

Method
Preheat the oven to 400°. In a large bowl combine all ingredients (except the pita bread) and mix with your hands until all ingredients are thoroughly combined. Do not overmix! Transfer to a medium saucepan and cook on medium heat for 20 minutes, then remove from heat. Arrange the pita halves on a parchment-lined baking sheet and fill each half with 3 tablespoons of the meat-pomegranate mixture while flattening it out with a spoon so the filling is even. Brush each pocket on both sides with a tiny bit of olive oil. Bake for 5 minutes. Remove from oven and let cool. Pita pockets should be browned and crispy.
Add the garnish on top of each pocket and serve.

Sima's Tip
The healthy fat found in pine nuts can help improve your satiety (the feeling you get when you feel full).

Egg Salad Cucumber Cups

These little "cups" are too adorable to not give a try. They are wonderful as hors d'oeuvres, an after-school snack, or as your post workout bite. The green onions add a strong flavor because they are raw in the recipe but won't be overpowering. The best things come in small packages, and these little bites come packed with huge flavor!

serves: 6 (makes 24 bites, 4 per serving)
prep: 10 cook: 12 total: 22
nut-free | dairy-free

Ingredients

4 whole hard boiled eggs + 2 egg whites, chopped
¼ cup chopped tarragon
¼ cup mayo (see recipe on page 189)
2 chopped green onions
2 tablespoon chopped dill
pinch of sea salt and black pepper (if you like it spicy, add 1 teaspoon of cayenne pepper)
3 large English cucumbers

Method

In a bowl, mix all ingredients except the cucumbers. Peel cucumbers and slice into thick rounds, about 2 inches each; 8 slices each cucumber). With a spoon scoop out the inside of each cucumber slice and arrange on a plate, facing up. Fill each cucumber slice with 1 tablespoon of egg salad.

Leggo My Tacos

Taco Tuesday? How about Tacos everyday! I love experimenting with the ingredients from beef to tofu, to guacamole, to all kinds of different veggies and salsas. In this recipe, I've gone with chicken tacos but gave it my own twist to liven up the traditional taco seasoning flavor. So, go ahead and snack on these tacos all day, every day!

serves: 4 (1 taco per serving)
prep: 10 cook: 0 total: 10
egg-free | nut-free | vegan option: replace chicken with tofu

Ingredients
2 boneless skinless cooked chicken breasts, thinly sliced
1 tablespoon sriracha sauce (more if you like it spicy)
4 sprouted corn tortillas, warmed
2 cups mixed white and purple cabbage, chopped
½ cup chopped cilantro
1 large avocado, quartered
juice from 1 lime

Method
Mix the chicken with sriracha sauce until all the pieces are well coated. Arrange warm tortillas on a plate and top with chopped cabbage and cilantro. Shred the spicy chicken and place on top of the cabbage. Top with more cilantro, avocado pieces, and drizzle with lime juice.

Sima's Tip
If you don't like spicy foods, eliminate the sriracha sauce. Alternatively, you can use store-bought mango salsa, pico de gallo, or even drizzle with raw tahini sauce.

Glutton Free Hash

Sweet potato hash is a dish that everyone should try. After trying this recipe, you will find yourself never eating hash browns any other way. This hash has the Healthy Indulgence twist without sacrificing the flavor of your traditional hash brown. You can enjoy this hash without feeling the gluttony, for sure.

serves: 4 (2 per serving)
prep: 10 cook: 10 total: 20
nut-free | dairy-free option: replace Greek yogurt with coconut yogurt

Ingredients
2 medium sweet potatoes
1 medium onion, peeled
2 eggs, beaten
3 tablespoons almond flour
1 teaspoon sea salt + pinch of ground pepper
pinch of cayenne pepper
coconut oil, for the pan

Savory Yogurt Sauce, option 1
1 cup 2% plain Greek yogurt (or coconut yogurt)
2 tablespoons green onions, chopped

Sweet Yogurt Sauce, option 2
1 cup 2% plain Greek yogurt (or coconut yogurt)
1 tablespoon pure maple syrup
1 tablespoon raw cacao nibs

Method
Wash and peel sweet potatoes. Shred the sweet potatoes and onion in a food processor or with a grater. Transfer to a kitchen towel and take out as much moisture as possible. In a large bowl, add the sweet potato and onion mixture, eggs, almond flour, sea salt, black pepper, and cayenne, and mix well. Melt 1 tablespoon of coconut oil in a large skillet over medium-high heat. With a spoon add to the hot skillet about 2–3 tablespoons of the sweet potato mixture and flatten just a little. Sauté for 2–3 minutes per side until golden brown and crispy. Transfer to a plate with paper towel on top. Serve warm with sweet or savory yogurt sauce.

Sima's Tip
Feel free to come up with your own sweet/savory combo for the yogurt sauce or try these unique flavors: cinnamon and chopped apples, harissa and chives, or lemon/lime zest with peppercorns. Will stay fresh in the refrigerator for 2–3 days, or in the freezer for up to 14 days.

So Berry-Coco-Licious

Warning: this is *not* your ordinary parfait! This is parfait-ing on a whole new level. The berry compote adds a sweet and dessert-like flavor. Just imagine all the layers of compote, granola, yogurt, and berries piled high and never ending. *Delicious.*

serves: 2 (1 cup per person)
prep: 10 cook: 0 total: 10
dairy-free | egg-free | vegan

Ingredients

Coconut Yogurt
2 cups fresh young Thai coconut meat
½ cup coconut water
1 pinch of sea salt
1 tablespoon lemon juice
Optional: ½ teaspoon probiotic powder (or you can empty 2 probiotic capsules instead)
2 tablespoons sweetener of choice (I use coconut nectar)

Parfait
1 cup granola (see recipe on page 62)
4 tablespoons berry compote (see recipe on page 58)
2 tablespoons unsweetened shredded coconut

Method
Add all coconut yogurt ingredients into a high-speed blender and blend for a few minutes until you get a silky-smooth texture. Set aside.

For the Parfait
In two tall martini glasses or mason jars, start layering your parfait with ½ cup granola in each cup, ¼ cup yogurt, 1 tablespoon berry compote, and repeat. Top with one tablespoon shredded coconut on top of each glass.

Sima's Tips
If you're crunched for time and making granola is out of the question, use any store-bought granola with ingredients that you can read and pronounce. I prefer the Purely Elizabeth brand. For added protein and omega-3s, add 1 teaspoon of chopped walnuts, cashews, or pistachios on top. Hey, why not go nuts?

Tuna, Lemme Upgrade Ya'!

If you're looking to upgrade your boring ol' canned tuna, look no further. In this recipe, the tuna is hit with a hint of cilantro, the acidity of lemon, and the creaminess of avocado. Not only will your taste buds do a happy dance, but the juice of the lemon can help your stomach with digestion. Move over plain ol' tuna, make room for a new and improved tuna recipe!

---

serves: 8 (½ avocado + 3 tablespoons tuna per serving)
prep: 10 cook: 0 total: 10
nut-free | dairy-free | egg-free

Ingredients
4 avocados, halved and pitted
3 (4.5-oz) cans tuna (in water or olive
    oil), drained
1 jalapeño, minced (remove seeds if you
    don't like it spicy)
1 cup cilantro, chopped
juice from 1 small lemon
pinch of sea salt and black pepper

Method
Scoop out the inside of the avocado. Place
the scooped avocado into a mixing bowl
and mash it with a fork. Then, add the
tuna, jalapeño, salt, pepper, lemon juice,
and cilantro to the mixing bowl. Stir it
all together until everything is mixed
thoroughly. Scoop the tuna mixture into
the avocado bowls.

Fava-Ful Beans

Mediterranean fava beans, originally called *foul medames* or *ful*, originated in Egypt. This recipe consists of fava beans, tahini sauce, spices, and hard-boiled eggs. Fava beans are not the most popular but they can be found as street food. They are rich in protein, fiber, and low in fat. It doesn't matter if they are fresh or canned, the health benefits remain the same and do your body good. Do your body a solid and include these magical beans in your diet.

serves: 2
prep: 0 cook: 30 total: 30
nut-free | dairy-free | egg-free option: omit eggs

Ingredients
2 cups (16 oz) canned fava beans
½ cup water
8 tablespoons raw tahini
juice from 2 fresh lemons
2 tablespoons extra-virgin olive oil
1 teaspoon cumin
⅛ teaspoon cayenne pepper
2 garlic cloves, chopped
salt and black pepper to taste

Toppings
sliced hard boiled eggs
¼ raw onion, sliced into rings (optional)
⅛ teaspooon of paprika
½ cup chopped parsley
¼ teaspoon red chili pepper flakes

Method
Place beans and water in a small saucepan on low-heat for about 3 minutes. Transfer to a bowl and add raw tahini, lemon juice, olive oil, cumin, cayenne, garlic, salt, and pepper. Stir beans and with a fork mash beans to chunky consistency. Divide onto 2 plates, top with eggs and onion (if using), then sprinkle with paprika, parsley, and red pepper flakes.

Lox Served Sweet

In this recipe, I've given lox on a bagel or cracker my Healthy Indulgence makeover. Instead of just serving the lox on a nutrient-empty carb, I used a sweet potato medallion. Makes the perfect post-workout or after-yoga snack packed with nutrients.

serves: 5 (2 rounds per person)
prep: 5 cook: 25 total: 30
nut-free | dairy-free | egg-free

Ingredients
1 large sweet potato
1–2 tablespoons olive or coconut oil
a few pinches of salt
2 slices lox (divided)
½ avocado, sliced
1 Persian cucumber, sliced
pinch of sea salt and black pepper

Method
Preheat oven to 400°. Wash potatoes and pat dry. Microwave sweet potatoes for 4 minutes. Lightly oil a baking sheet. Slice sweet potato lengthwise into ¼-inch rounds. Coat both sides of sweet potato with oil and lightly sprinkle with salt. Cook for 15 minutes (flip after the first 10 minutes). Set oven to broil and continue to cook for an additional minute on each side, until toasted. Top with lox, avocado, cucumber, and sprinkle with black pepper.

Diff' from the Rest Dip

The protein alone in these beans will keep you full and going all day long. This not-so-ordinary dip tops all black bean dips out there because of the addition of the superfoods black garlic and ginger. Not only will you be enjoying each dip and bite you take, but your body will thank you by saying: give me more of this awesome dip.

serves: 4 (1 quarter pita + 2 tablespoon of dip for each person)
prep: 10 cook: 0 total: 10
nut-free | dairy-free

Ingredients
2 black garlic cloves, chopped
1 teaspoon extra-virgin olive oil
3 tablespoons water
1-inch fresh ginger
1 (15.5-oz) can no salt added black beans, drained
juice of 1 lime
1 tablespoon extra-virgin olive oil
1 100% whole wheat pita bread cut into quarters

Method
Sauté the garlic in olive oil until lightly browned. After garlic is sautéed, add garlic and rest of ingredients (except pita bread) in high-speed blender or food processor and blend until all ingredients mix together (if mixture is too thick, add a little more water). To serve, spread 2 tablespoons of black bean dip on each pita quarter.

For the Pita Chips
Toast your pita chips twice to give them a really crunchy texture.

Sauces

How do you make sauces? They're easy to prepare with the variety of fresh, healthy ingredients that elevate the taste of your food and add nourishment to your body. It should be noted that it's better to create a fresh sauce from scratch than to get packaged, processed sauce from the store. Many of the recipes in this book have sauces included, so start your sauce-making journey on the next few pages and learn how to prepare delicious sauces that pair well with any of your Healthy Indulgence recipes.

SAUCE RECIPES

No-Egg-Mayonaiz-ey

Garbanzo beans are not only used to make hummus, they have a whole host of uses. In this case, they shine in my eggless mayo. Try it out today and make it a permanent addition to the condiments section of your refrigerator. It's light, nutritious, and definitely better than your store-bought mayo. FYI: this recipe will only work using an immersion blender.

makes: 1 cup
prep: 5 cook: 0 total: 5
egg-free | nut-free | dairy-free | vegan

Ingredients
4 tablespoons liquid from 1 can of low sodium chickpeas (a.k.a. aquafaba)
1 teaspoon Dijon mustard
1 tablespoon lemon juice
½ teaspoon sea salt
1 cup grapeseed oil (do not use olive oil)

Flavored Mayo Options
Mediterranean: a pinch of saffron
Spicy: add ½ teaspoon sriracha
Herb: Add 1 teaspoon of dried herbs of your choice such as herbes de Provence, basil, rosemary, or thyme

Method
In a tall jar add the chickpea water, Dijon mustard, lemon juice, and sea salt. Place the immersion blender inside the tall jar and slowly start adding the oil. Blend for 1–2 minutes or until liquid thickens and becomes white in color.

Sima's Tip
To keep fresh, store in an airtight container and keep refrigerated for up to 5 days.

Sima's Tip
When ready to serve, drizzle with oil and top with chopped parsley or caramelized onions. To keep freshness, store in an airtight container in the refrigerator for up to 3 days.

Mommy's Hummus

Mom's secret is using some of the aquafaba that comes with canned chickpeas. It adds a most unique, special flavor that sets this hummus above the rest. Thanks, Mom!

makes: 1 cup
prep: 5 cook: 0 total: 5
egg-free | nut-free | dairy-free | vegan

Ingredients
1 (15-oz) can low sodium chickpeas or 1½ cups cooked chickpeas
juice from 1 small lemon
¼ cup raw tahini
1 small garlic clove
½ teaspoon ground cumin
½ teaspoon sea salt
3–5 tablespoons water + 2 tablespoons chickpea liquid (add more or less for consistency desired)

To Garnish
pinch of ground paprika
1 tablespoon olive oil
3 tablespoons chopped parsley

Method
Save 2 tablespoons of chickpea liquid, then rinse chickpeas. Place all ingredients in a high-speed blender and blend until smooth. Depending on desired consistency, add or subtract water (less water will be more creamy).

Happy Belly Hummus

Black garlic is the secret to create unmatched flavor here, but that's not all. Being a fermented food it supplies the "good" bacteria you need to have a happy and healthy gut. I enjoy using Sadaf's Black Garlic as it always is the most aromatic.

makes: 1 cup
prep: 5 cook: 0 total: 5
egg-free | nut-free | dairy-free | vegan

Ingredients
1 (15-oz) can low sodium chickpeas or 1½ cups cooked chickpeas
juice from 1 small lemon
¼ cup raw tahini
half a head of black garlic
½ teaspoon ground cumin
½ teaspoon sea salt
3–5 tablespoons water + 2 tablespoons chickpea liquid (add more or less for consistency)
1 tablespoon olive oil, for serving

Optional
Caramelized onions, for serving

Method
Rinse chickpeas from can, reserving 2 tablespoons of the liquid. Place all ingredients in a high-speed blender and blend until smooth. Depending on desired consistency, add or subtract water (more water will be watery, less water will be more creamy).

Better than Brownie Spread

Dense, fudgy, and utterly delicious is the only way to describe this hummus dip with an unexpected chocolately twist—on top of being scrumptious, it is also high in anti-oxidants from the cacao. So, drop that brownie full of sugar and try this wholesome dip instead.

makes: 1 cup

prep: 5 cook: 0 total: 5

egg-free | dairy-free | vegan

Ingredients

1 (15-oz) can low sodium chickpeas
5 tablespoons unsweetened cacao powder
½ cup vegan chocolate chips
¼ cup pure maple syrup
½ teaspoon sea salt
1 pinch cinnamon
1 tablespoon vanilla extract
¼ cup unsweetened nondairy milk (almond, coconut, or cashew)
Fresh strawberries, to serve

Method

Add all the ingredients (except milk and strawberries) to high-speed blender. Blend until smooth, while adding in the milk to thin out to your desired consistency.

Sima's Tip

For extra yumminess, serve with fresh strawberries. To keep fresh, store in airtight container in the refrigerator for up to 2–3 days.

Muhammara

Here's how you pronounce this sauce: moo-hahm-MRAH. This typical Moroccan sauce is tart and a little nutty due to the walnuts and the pomegranate molasses. Pomegranate molasses is made of two ingredients: pomegranate juice and lemon juice. The muhammara can be compared to hummus in its versatility, but tastes very different. If you're looking for a change from hummus, this sauce is a great alternative.

makes: 1½ cups
prep: 10 cook: 15 total: 25
egg-free | *dairy-free* | *vegan*

Ingredients

2 red bell peppers
1 cup walnuts, toasted
1 clove garlic, roughly chopped
juice of ½ lemon
¼ cup 100% whole wheat bread
    crumbs
1 tablespoon pomegranate molasses
1 teaspoon paprika
½ teaspoon red pepper flakes
pinch of cumin
2 tablespoons olive oil

Method

Line a baking sheet with tin foil and place halved red peppers on it, skin side up. Broil peppers until skins are charred. Set aside and let peppers cool. As soon as peppers are cool to touch, remove charred skins. Add all ingredients into a high-speed blender except for olive oil. While blending, add in olive oil to incorporate with the mixture and blend until desired consistency.

Sima's Tip

Pair with any of my healthy indulgence sandwiches or as a snack with 100% whole wheat pita or naan bread. To keep fresh, store in an airtight container in the refrigerator for 3–5 days.

Pink Coconut Sauce

Pink peppercorns aren't actually peppercorns, but a berry from a Peruvian tree. Replace your fat- and cholesterol-loaded jar of mayo with this delicate sauce full of antioxidants and a soft pink hue.

makes: 2½ cups
prep: 5 cook: 0 total: 5
egg-free | nut-free | dairy-free | vegan

Ingredients
1 clove garlic, peeled
½ teaspoon sea salt, plus more to taste
1 tablespoon pink peppercorns (if using black peppercorns, use ½ tablespoon)
1 tablespoon extra-virgin olive oil
1 small bunch of chives, chopped
½ cup finely chopped cilantro
1 (14-oz) can of coconut milk (full fat)
3 tablespoons lemon juice

Method
In a mortar and pestle, grind garlic, salt, and peppercorns into a paste. Then add oil, chives, and cilantro, continuing to form paste. Pour mixture in a bowl and mix in coconut milk, creating a smooth sauce. Add lemon juice and mix well.

Sima's Tip
To keep fresh, store in an airtight container in refrigerator for up to 5 days.

Cheese-less Pesto

Lose the cheese, not the nuts. Pine nuts, that is, as they are known to suppress appetite and boost energy. Try this pesto with my sandwiches, soups, and any of the salads. You won't even miss the cheese!

makes: 1 cup
prep: 7 cook: 0 total: 7
egg-free | dairy-free | vegan

Ingredients
2 garlic cloves
juice of 1 large lemon
1 cup packed fresh basil leaves
1 cup packed fresh parsley
½ cup low sodium canned chickpeas
3 tablespoons nutritional yeast
¼ cup olive oil
¼ cup walnut halves, lightly toasted (until golden in color)
¼ cup pine nuts, lightly toasted (until golden in color)
sprinkle of sea salt and pepper

Method
Add all ingredients to a high-speed blender and process until desired consistency (either smooth or chunky). To keep fresh, store in an airtight container in refrigerator for 3–5 days.

Sima's Tip
Nutritional yeast is different from the yeast you use in baking because it doesn't foam or froth. It's also high in vitamin B_{12} and contains iron and is often used by vegans as an alternative to dairy products.

Granny's Marinara

In the good ol' days, Grandma would spend hours making a delicious marinara to enjoy with pasta and meatballs. Nowadays I don't have hours to spend in the kitchen, but I get an equally delicious sauce in under 30 minutes and presto, time to eat. Use it on my sandwiches, Skinny Minny Meatballs (page 76), and even zoodles.

---

makes: 2–3 cups
prep: 5 cook: 25 total: 30
egg-free | nut-free | dairy-free | vegan

Ingredients
2 tablespoons olive oil
1 medium onion, minced
½ cup carrots, chopped
2 black garlic cloves, chopped
2 garlic cloves, minced
1 (24-oz) can crushed tomatoes
1 (15-oz) can diced tomatoes
1 teaspoon each: sea salt, dried basil, and
    dried oregano
¼ teaspoon red chili flakes
fresh basil, for garnish

Method
In a large saucepan over medium heat, add olive oil and onion and sauté for 3 minutes, until translucent. Add carrots, both garlics, and sauté for another 2 minutes. Add remaining ingredients and spices, reduce heat, and simmer for another 20 minutes. Remove from heat and let cool.

Sima's Tip
To keep fresh, store in an airtight container in refrigerator for up to 5 days.

Sips

In this section, you will find recipes for satisfying tonics, lattes, and delicious juice blends that are loaded with superfoods, antioxidants, and anti-inflammatory nutrients such as my Power Goji Tea and Elegant Pomegranate. While water is the most important liquid you should be drinking—and you should be drinking at least 8 glasses of water per day—there are other drinks you can make that are equally nutritious but more delicious and refreshing that you will find in the upcoming pages. These "Sips" recipes comprise a big part of all my clients' food plans and I encourage you to add them too. To your health— Cheers, Salud, L'chayim, Skol, Kanpai!

SIPS RECIPES

Power Goji Tea

My clients know that when they start their healthy indulgence plan, they will have my warm goji lemon tea to drink first thing in the morning. The ingredients pack a powerful punch with anti-inflammatory, antioxidant, and anti-infective properties. Four ingredients, five minutes, and thousands of benefits all in one cleansing drink.

serves: 2
prep: 0 cook: 5 total: 5
nut-free | dairy-free | egg-free | vegan

Ingredients
2 cups hot water
juice of 2 small lemons
2 tablespoon goji berries
½ teaspoon sweetener of choice (optional)

Method
Add lemon juice to the water. Then add goji berries and allow goji berries to sit for 5 minutes to rehydrate and infuse water. Add your sweetener if using, and enjoy.

Sima's Tip
After drinking the goji tea, you may also eat the goji berries because they are softer and easier for your body to digest.

Chocolaty Goodness

What do you need when it's too cold? A nice warm cup of creamy, chocolaty goodness that is my best *ever* hot cocoa. Add to that maca powder, turmeric, and a pinch of cayenne, and you have a decadent cocoa that is on superfood steroids.

serves: 2
prep: 2 cook: 5 total: 7
egg-free | *dairy-free* | *vegan*

Ingredients
2 cups unsweetened almond milk
1 tablespoon coconut oil
1 tablespoon unsweetened cacao powder
½ teaspoon raw maca powder
½ teaspoon turmeric
½ tablespoon pure maple syrup
2 dashes cinnamon
pinch of cayenne
pinch of sea salt

Method
Warm milk on stove over medium heat for 5 minutes. Remove from heat and add all ingredients to a high-speed blender and blend on high for 2 minutes.

Turmeric Latte

This latte is creamy and heavy with the aroma of cinnamon and ginger. The addition of black pepper is a necessary component to this drink, not for the flavor aspect but for the chemical breakdown of the turmeric so our bodies can absorb it properly. Turmeric does a body good!

serves: 2
prep: 5 cook: 5 total: 10
egg-free | dairy-free | vegan

Ingredients

2 cups unsweetened almond or coconut milk
2 tablespoons fresh turmeric root, grated
2 teaspoons cinnamon
2 tablespoons grated fresh ginger (or 1 teaspoon ground)
2 teaspoons coconut oil
2 teaspoons coconut nectar or sweetener of your choice
2 pinches black pepper

Method

Warm the almond or coconut milk in a small saucepan over medium-low heat. Do not let it burn. Warm through for 2–3 minutes. Add turmeric root, cinnamon, ginger, and black pepper. Then combine coconut oil with the mixture and gently heat together until melted. Stir for 2 minutes or until frothy. Lastly, stir in coconut nectar or sweetener of choice to taste.

Mocha Boost

Who doesn't love chocolate in the morning? Even more so when there is a viable benefit in your morning drink? In this recipe, we have reishi mushrooms, an edible fungus also known as one of the original superfoods. Some of the beneficial properties include better immune function, mental clarity, and increased longevity. If that's the case, make mine a double.

serves: 2
prep: 2 cook: 4 total: 6
egg-free | nut-free | dairy-free | vegan

Ingredients

2 cups of coffee
1 tablespoon unsweetened cacao powder
1 tablespoon reishi mushroom powder
½ teaspoon cinnamon
2 teaspoons sweetener of your choice

Method

Combine all ingredients in a high-speed blender for 1–2 minutes. Pour ingredients into a saucepan and warm through for 3–4 minutes. Serve and top with raw cacao nibs.

Limonana

There is a small place in my home town that is a hole in the wall where people stand in line for hours just to get a dose of this limonana. Limonana is a combination of two words: Limon and Nana—which translates into lemon and mint. Mint is so beneficial in the fact that it serves as a palate cleanser, promotes digestion, and helps to soothe stomachs in case of indigestion. To maximize health benefits, I recommend you use Kangen Water—my absolute favorite brand is Health And Wealth Lovers (you can find in the resources section).

serves: 2

prep: 5 cook: 0 total: 5

nut-free | egg-free | dairy-free | vegan

Ingredients
¾ cup of water

½ cup fresh lemon juice

4 stems worth of mint leaves with the stems discarded, plus a few extra sprigs for garnish if desired

2 teaspoons sweetener of your choice (coconut nectar or coconut sugar)

10–20 ice cubes

Method
Add all ingredients to high-speed blender. Pulse a few times to create the consistency of a slushy.

Pour into glasses, garnish with mint leaves if desired, and serve immediately.

Elegant Pomegranate

Are you ready to make an impact at your next gathering? Make this drink that has a beautiful red hue, and a flavor that is nothing like many have experienced. The secret ingredient is the rose water, which is made from steeping rose petals in water. Talk about refined and elegant in a glass.

serves: 2
prep: 5 cook: 0 total: 5
nut-free | egg-free | dairy-free | vegan

Ingredients
2 teaspoons pomegranate molasses
16 ounces sparkling water
2 tablespoons pomegranate arils
5–10 ice cubes
1 teaspoon rose water

Method
Add all ingredients to pitcher and mix until pomegranate molasses dissolves. Add the pomegranate arils and serve.

Cleansing Cardamom Tea

When preparing the ingredients for this tea, you'll feel like you are in a spice market with the aromas of the cardamom pods, star anise, cinnamon, and ginger. Cardamom and ginger are actually related in the sense that both are used to prevent digestive problems, fighting nausea, bloating, and heartburn.

serves: 2
prep: 5 cook: 10 total: 15
nut-free | egg-free | dairy-free | vegan

Ingredients
4 cardamom pods
4 black peppercorns
2 star anise
1 cinnamon stick
4 slices fresh ginger
2 teaspoons coconut nectar

Method
Place all ingredients in 2½ cups of water, warm through for 15 minutes but do not boil, and then strain. Add any extra sweetener desired, and serve.

Lavender Coconut Lemonade

Lemonade on its own is great, but let's give it a boost with coconut water and then infuse it with the subtle flavor of lavender. Lavender is well known for the relaxing effect it gives. I enjoy using Health And Wealth Lovers' Kangen Water in this lemonade! Sit back, grab a glass, and enjoy a good book or the company of a loved one.

---

serves: 12
prep: 15 cook: 0 total: 15
egg-free | nut-free | dairy-free | vegan

Ingredients
1¾ cups coconut sugar
6 cups water
1½ cups fresh squeezed lemon juice
6 cups coconut water
½ cup Lavender Simple Syrup (see below for recipe)

Lavender Simple Syrup
2 cups coconut sugar
1½ cups water
3 tablespoons dried lavender

Method
Mix coconut sugar and water and stir until sugar is completely dissolved. Add lemon juice and coconut water and stir until combined. Add lavender simple syrup to mixture and combine until you reach desired sweetness. Add ice and serve.

For the Lavender Simple Syrup
Combine the coconut sugar, water, and lavender in a medium saucepan. Bring to a boil for 2 minutes.

Remove from heat and let lavender infuse the syrup for 15 minutes (or more if you would like a stronger flavor). Once cooled, strain and set aside.

Apple Cinnamon Water

H_2O is the best thing on Earth, but if you're looking to change it up, try this water that is bursting with the flavors of apple and cinnamon. Not only do you get the gratification of drinking flavorful water, but you also have the benefit of cinnamon that helps reduce heart disease, lower blood sugar, and strengthen your immunity.

serves: 6–8
prep: 5 cook: 15 total: 20
nut-free | egg-free | dairy-free | vegan

Ingredients
8 cups water
2–3 medium apples (Fuji, Gala, or Pink Lady)
3 cinnamon sticks

Method
Bring water to quick boil and reduce heat to simmer. Core and slice apples. Add apples and cinnamon sticks to water. Simmer 15 minutes on medium low heat. Strain water into glass pitcher. Add ice or refrigerate.

Sparkling Rose-Berry

This drink is fancy enough to serve at a weekend brunch, but easy enough to make regularly at home. Berries are the star to this drink because they are antioxidant powerhouses. Also, the array of berries adds a rainbow of beautiful color to your diet.

---

serves: 4
prep: 5 cook: 0 total: 5
egg-free | nut-free | dairy-free | vegan

Ingredients
2 cups raspberries, blackberries, or berries of your choice (optional: add 2 teaspoons of chia seeds to berries)

4 cups sparkling water

4 tablespoons rosemary syrup (see recipe below)

2 sprigs of rosemary, leaves picked (for garnish)

4 lime wheels for garnish

Rosemary Simple Syrup
½ cup coconut sugar

1½ cups water

3 tablespoons dried rosemary

Method
Gently smash berries in a mortar and pestle until almost completely crushed, leaving a few chunks for texture. Pour sparkling water into a pitcher and combine with rosemary syrup. Divide and add muddled berries into bottoms of cups. Pour sparkling water and rosemary syrup mixture into cups, add ice, and garnish with lime wheels and rosemary sprigs.

For the Rosemary Simple Syrup
Combine the coconut sugar, water, and rosemary in a medium saucepan. Bring to a boil for 1 minute. Remove from heat and let rosemary infuse the syrup for 15 minutes (or more if you would like a stronger flavor). Once cooled, strain and set aside for use.

Homemade Coconut Mylk

With a creamy texture and slight sweetness, it tastes like more of an indulgent drink than a healthy alternative to regular milk. The "special" factor to this mylk is that it is made in just ten minutes, what's easier than that? Coconut mylk can help lower cholesterol, improve blood pressure, and it contains lauric acid, which is a beneficial fat that helps to improve energy.

serves: 4–6
prep: 5 cook: 5 total: 10
nut-free | egg-free | dairy-free | vegan

Ingredients
4 cups water or coconut water (I use Harmless Harvest coconut water)
1½–2 cups shredded coconut

Method
In a saucepan, heat water or coconut water, but do not let it boil! Keep it on a rolling simmer for 5 minutes. Remove from heat. Pour coconut in high-speed blender and add warmed water. Blend on high for 3 minutes or until a creamy texture.

Pour through a mesh sieve (or a cheesecloth) to get the most water out of the mixture. Then place mixture in multiple layers of cheesecloth and extract remaining liquid out of the coconut. Drink immediately or store in the fridge. Will stay fresh in refrigerator for up to 3 days. Separation may occur; just shake before serving.

Sweets

The enemy of all diets. The guilt master of our lives. The reason many Americans go to the gym every Monday. Who among us can resist the sweet temptation of a decadent, warm, oozing chocolate lava cake? While most diets will not allow you to even think about such things, *Sima's Healthy Indulgence* encourages you to indulge—provided you do so adhering to recipes in this chapter. In this section, you will find Chocolate Dreamy Tart, Nice Cream, "Begging for More" Cheesecake, and even my favorite—Super Bark, good for you and delicious, à la Sima.

Find a reason to indulge!

SWEETS RECIPES

I Scream, U Scream, Nice Cream

If ice cream is your weakness, I have a very nice treat for you. "Nice cream" is frozen bananas blended up until it has the texture of soft serve. The best part? You get to choose what goes into the ice cream. It's like having your own ice cream shop in your kitchen. This treat is just as yummy as ice cream but without the need for added sugar. Shhhh . . . don't tell anyone it's healthy.

---

serves: 4
prep: 10 cook: 0 total: 10
egg-free | dairy-free | nut-free | vegan

Ingredients

4 ripe frozen bananas, halved
1 tablespoon unsweetened cocoa powder
¼ teaspoon pure vanilla extract
2 tablespoons sweet cacao nibs

Method

Place frozen bananas in a high-speed blender and blend until you achieve the consistency of soft serve ice cream. Pour the banana puree into a bowl and mix in the rest of the ingredients until thoroughly combined. Cover the bowl and place in freezer for another 20 minutes. Remove and scoop out into bowls.

Super Bark

Do you have chocolate cravings? I have the solution for you. This ridiculously easy, no-bake treat is full of superfood goodness and delicious spices. This recipe is not only gorgeous, but it screams holiday spirit and is perfect to give as a gift (if you haven't eaten it all yourself already). The goji berries and pistachios add an extra element of antioxidants and friendly fats. It is not only delectable and healthy, but it satisfies your sweet craving in a matter of minutes.

---

makes: 8–10 barks
prep: 10 cook: 5 total: 15
egg-free | dairy-free | vegan

Ingredients
1 cup coconut oil, melted
⅔ cup unsweetened cacao powder
2 tablespoons almond butter
2 tablespoons coconut sugar
1 pinch ground cardamom
1 pinch cinnamon
1 pinch sea salt

Optional Toppings
raw pistachios
edible flowers
cacao nibs
goji berries
shredded coconut
mulberries

Method
Warm coconut oil to liquefy (if it is in a hardened form, place in a container with warm water until it turns to liquid). Once coconut oil is liquefied, mix in all ingredients thoroughly. Move your chocolate bark mixture to a parchment-lined baking sheet and spread evenly to make sure you get an even layer for your bark. Add your toppings of choice and place in freezer until completely hardened.

Sima's Tips
To break apart bark, you can lift the whole sheet from pan and break by hands. If you have a nut allergy, feel free to substitute your favorite seed butter instead—hemp or sunflower butter are a great options here.

Sinfully Yours Cookies

Of course cookies are supposed to be sinful. But these are not just sinful, they are healthful as well. These PCF-certified cookies will swiftly carry you at your best throughout the day. So go ahead, commit some cookie sins. Do it with passion. It's what Sima ordered.

makes: 12 cookies
prep: 10 cook: 15 total: 25
dairy-free | nut-free option: omit nut butter and use seed butter instead

Ingredients
2 cups quick oats
½ teaspoon baking powder
½ teaspoon baking soda
¾ teaspoon cinnamon
½ teaspoon sea salt
½ cup raw almond butter or cashew butter
1 teaspoon pure vanilla extract
1 egg
2 tablespoons lemon zest + 1 tablespoon lemon juice
3 tablespoons maple syrup
1 cup bananas, mashed (about 3 medium bananas)
¼ cup poppy seeds

Method
Preheat oven to 350°. Line a baking sheet with parchment paper and spray with cooking spray. In a large bowl add oats, baking powder, baking soda, sea salt, and cinnamon, and whisk. Add your choice of nut butter to vanilla extract, egg, lemon zest, lemon juice, maple syrup, mashed bananas, and poppy seeds, and mix until all ingredients come together. With the palm of your hands, form 12 cookies and spread them out on your prepared baking sheet. With a spoon, gently flatten the top of each cookie and bake for 15 minutes. Remove from oven and allow cookies to cool.

Sima's Tip
If you are not a fan of poppy seeds, feel free to substitute to white or black chia seeds instead, or completely eliminate them from recipe.

Chocolate Dreamy Tart

Here is a no-bake, decadent, elegant, too-good-to-be-true dessert that will keep your guests begging for more. I love using raw cacao powder as it has four times the antioxidant power of regular dark chocolate and contains protein, calcium, carotene, magnesium, and sulfur. I love garnishing this dreamy tart with pomegranate arils as it adds a tarty taste and looks divine.

---

makes: 10 slices
prep: 20 cook: 0 total: 20
egg-free | dairy-free | vegan

Ingredients

Crust
2 cups mixed pecans and walnuts
1 cup pitted Medjool dates, chopped
2 tablespoons coconut oil
1 teaspoon maca powder
2 teaspoons cinnamon

Chocolate Filling
2 cups raw cashew pieces
1 tablespoon vanilla extract
½ cup coconut oil, melted
¼ cup cacao butter
⅓ cup nectar or maple syrup
8 tablespoons pomegranate juice
¾ cup raw cacao powder

Garnish
Pomegranate arils

Method
Pulse all crust ingredients in a high-speed blender until the crust is combined and looks like a paste. Remove from blender, mix with your hands for 2 more minutes, and press into a springform (8-inch) pan into an even layer all around. Place in refrigerator or freezer to set. Next, take all the ingredients for the filling and place in high-speed blender and combine thoroughly. Remove crust from refrigerator and pour chocolate filling on top. Place in freezer until tart sets. Garnish with pomegranate arils and serve. Will stay fresh in your fridge for up to 7 days.

Sima's Tip
Feel free to garnish with any berry of your choice.

Blushing Rose Sorbet

This recipe contains one of my favorites: rose water. Besides adding special anti-inflammatory properties, rose water gives a very distinct floral nature to this recipe. My favorite rose water is by Sadaf, as it's very floral. This sorbet is not only light and refreshing, but good for your body and skin. Refreshing and rejuvenating.

serves: 4
prep: 10 cook: 0 total: 10
egg-free | dairy-free | nut-free | vegan

Ingredients
½ cup coconut sugar
zest and flesh of 1 lemon (make sure to
    not have any of the seeds in the flesh
    otherwise it will make the sorbet bitter)
2¼ cups fresh strawberries
4 cups ice
1 tablespoon rose water
3 tablespoons water

Optional
1 more cup of water (to make sorbet more
    slushy)

Method
In a high-speed blender, put in coconut sugar and lemon zest and mix. Next, add strawberries and lemon flesh and blend for 2 minutes. Then add ice and rose water. Blend all ingredients until it forms a slush. You can use the optional water to make sorbet more slushy.

Sima's Tip
Serve in plates or glasses. Serve immediately or place in freezer to chill.

Chocoholic Cups

When it comes to giving a healthy indulgent makeover, chocolate recipes are my favorite to revamp. It's about time we combined two of our biggest guilty pleasures and make one kick-ass dessert. The almonds in this recipe are a rich supply of MUFAs (monounsaturated fatty acids), which are a healthy type of fat. This dessert is seriously to die for.

---

makes: 6 large or 9 mini cups

prep: 20 cook: 5 total: 25

egg-free | dairy-free | vegan

Ingredients

Dark Chocolate Cups

4 cups water

18 oz dairy free dark chocolate chips

2 tablespoons coconut oil, melted

3 tablespoons maple syrup

Cookie Dough Filling
Option #1:

1 cup raw almonds

¼ cup coconut flour (almond flour can be substituted)

½ cup almond butter

2½ cups pitted Medjool dates

Option #2:

1 cup almonds (or your favorite nuts)

½ cup low sodium chickpeas

½ cup old-fashioned oats, finely ground

¼ cup coconut oil, melted

¼ cup maple syrup

¾ teaspoon pure vanilla extract

⅓ cup unsalted nut butter

½ teaspoon cinnamon

¼ teaspoon ground cardamom (optional)

2–3 teaspoons water

Method

Prepare muffin tin with paper liners. In a small pot, boil 4 cups of water on medium-high heat (or use a double-boiler) and place a microwave-safe bowl on top, then pour dark chocolate chips into bowl. Stir constantly until chocolate is melted. When melted, combine with the coconut oil and maple syrup. Continue to stir. Reserve half the mixture for later, then pour melted chocolate mixture into each liner in the muffin tin until filled halfway. Place in the freezer to harden for roughly 10–15 minutes.

Next, take all the ingredients for the cookie dough filling of your choice and pulse in a high-speed blender until broken down like a paste or "cookie dough." Transfer to a bowl and knead with your hands to incorporate all ingredients. Take 2 tablespoons of the dough and place on top of the hardened chocolate. Then, take the remaining melted chocolate mixture and pour on top of each cookie, filling up the liner evenly. Let set in freezer for another 10–15 minutes to ensure all the chocolate has hardened and the entire cup is solid.

Quickie Cookie

These cookies really are the best thing ever! Straight from the oven they are soft, chewy, and will make your house smell amazing! The best part is, it doesn't even need any flour and it only takes 15 minutes to bake, so if you ever need to make a batch of cookies for your guests, this will be your go-to!

makes: 15 cookies
prep: 10 cook: 15 total: 25
dairy-free | nut-free

Ingredients
1 cup old-fashioned rolled oats + 1 cup oat flour
½ teaspoon baking powder
½ teaspoon baking soda
¼ cup + 2 tablespoons coconut oil, melted
½ cup coconut nectar (or sweetener of your choice)
2 eggs
1 teaspoon pure vanilla extract

Add-ins
¾ cup dairy free dark chocolate chips or chocolate chunks (70% or more cocoa)

Method
Preheat oven to 350° and line a baking sheet with parchment paper. In a medium bowl, whisk together all the dry ingredients and set aside. In another medium bowl, whisk together all the wet ingredients. Add the dry ingredients to the wet ingredients and whisk until all ingredients are mixed thoroughly. Next, add in your chocolate chips and gently mix together. With the palm of your hands, form small balls and place on your baking sheet. With the back of a spoon flatten each ball to get a round shape cookie and bake for 15 minutes. Remove from oven and let it cool for 5 minutes.

Berry Nice Froyo

So you've had a long day and want to treat yourself to a little frozen refreshment. I have for you a unique and sweet treat. This frozen yogurt cup is a cool and refreshing dessert that's actually beneficial to your body. Delicious creaminess from the coconut yogurt and a tasty crunch from the granola makes this dessert berry nice.

---

serves: 4

prep: 20 cook: 0 total: 20

egg-free | nut-free option: replace almond butter with seed butter

---

Ingredients
2 tablespoons unsalted almond butter
1 cup granola (recipe on page 62)
2 cups 2% plain Greek yogurt (or use coconut yogurt)
1 cup fresh mixed berries, halved (strawberries, blueberries, or raspberries)

Optional
2 tablespoons maple syrup

Method
Place the almond butter in a microwave-safe bowl and melt for 30 seconds. Once melted, pour in granola and mix thoroughly. Place ¼ of a cup of the granola mixture at the bottom of a mini glass bowl and press to create an even layer. Add a ½ cup of the yogurt on top of the granola mixture, and transfer to freezer and allow to freeze for 15 minutes. Remove from freezer and top with berries, and drizzle with maple syrup.

"Begging for More" Cheesecake

This recipe has been taste-tested and heartily approved by my teenage daughter, who, trust me, is a tough critic. It is delicately sweet and rustic, yet decadently desserty, and packed with energy and antioxidants. After a slice, you would be getting seconds . . . it's okay, its approved.

makes: 8–10 slices
prep: 20 cook: 0 total: 20
dairy-free | egg-free | vegan

Ingredients

Crust
1 cup raw walnuts
1 cup raw macadamia nuts
½ cup pitted Medjool dates
¼ cup dried unsweetened coconut

Filling
3 cups chopped cashews (soaked in water overnight)
¾ cup fresh squeezed lemon juice
¾ cup coconut nectar
¾ cup extra-virgin cold pressed coconut oil
1 teaspoon vanilla extract
½ teaspoon sea salt
½ cup water

Raspberry Sauce
2 cups frozen raspberries (or any berry of your choice)
1 teaspoon rose water
2 pitted Medjool dates

Method

For the Crust
In a high-speed blender process all ingredients until a paste is made. Cover the bottom of an 8-inch springform pan with the crust and press in to form an even layer.

For the Filling
In a high-speed blender, add the pre-soaked cashews, lemon juice, coconut nectar, coconut oil, vanilla, sea salt, and ½ cup water until smooth. Pour the filling on top of the crust. Place the cake in the freezer to firm up.

For the Raspberry Sauce
Put raspberries in high-speed blender; process with the rose water and pitted dates to make sauce to garnish cake.

Sima's Tip
To keep fresh, freeze cheesecake and remove from freezer 15 minutes before ready to serve. Re-freeze the leftover.

Maple Nutty Pears

Roasted pears with cinnamon, maple syrup, and walnuts—it doesn't get simpler than this. The aroma of roasted sweet pears filling your home is very welcoming and makes it a treat you can't resist. Such a big statement for a humble fruit, right? They're a prime example of how simple, good-for-you, and *real* whole foods can be merged together to produce an indulging dessert that's healthy for the whole family to devour.

serves: 4
prep: 5 cook: 25 total: 30
egg-free | *dairy-free* | *vegan* | *nut-free option: omit walnuts*

Ingredients
2 large ripe pears
¼ cup crushed walnuts
¼ teaspoon ground cinnamon
4 tablespoons maple syrup or
    coconut nectar

Method
Preheat oven to 350°. Cut pears in half, then using a melon baller cut out and remove center with seeds and place on baking sheet. Fill pear with crushed walnuts, drizzle maple syrup over the entire pear, and dust with cinnamon. Place in oven and bake for 20 minutes or until tender.

Sima's Tip
You can use apples or quinces instead of the pears. Pronounced "kwins," the quince is a small and rounded pome fruit grown on trees. Bitter when they are raw, so they need to be cooked or roasted.

Sima's 3-Day Healthy Indulgence Detox Plan

I've created this detox plan using recipes from this book that are plant-based, egg-free, dairy-free, sugar-free, and full of nutrients to give you the boost and energy you need during your detox. As you already know by now, I don't believe in or promote any extreme plans, especially detox plans that contain only juicing or only liquids or that are extremely low in calories.

I use this detox plan myself when I feel bloated, or when I overeat or overindulge. In fact, this is a perfect plan to start right after the holidays. You can extend it to 4 or 5 days, and feel free to mix and match the meal suggestions provided between the days. As I always say: it's on your terms. When I follow this plan, I notice that I don't get hungry, and I feel full and satisfied after every meal.

Day 1

First: Power Goji Tea (page 191)

Breakfast: Almond Oats To-Go (page 63)

AM Snack: 2 Cherry Tahini Exercise Bites (page 153)

Lunch: Full-Filling Butternut Squash Soup (page 100)

PM Snack: 4 tablespoons Fueled Up Trail Mix (page 150) + 1 medium apple

Dinner: Cleansing Tabbouleh Salad (page 109)

After Dinner: Chamomile tea or caffeine-free mint tea

Day 2

First: Power Goji Tea (page 191)

Breakfast: Green Tea Detox Smoothie (page 54)

AM Snack: Positivity Smoothie (page 149)

Lunch: Za'atar Chickpea Pocket (page 73)

PM Snack: 2 Cherry Tahini Exercise Bites (page 153)

Dinner: Day at the spa salad (omit chicken) (page 191)

After Dinner: Chamomile tea or caffeine-free mint tea

Day 3

First: Power Goji Tea (page 191)

Breakfast: Rejuvenation Bowl (page 43)

AM Snack: 4 tablespoons Fueled Up Trail Mix (page 150) + 1 medium apple

Lunch: Weekday Earth Detox Soup (page 96)

PM Snack: 1 pear + 1 small Persian cucumber

Dinner: Party It Up Salad (omit feta) (page 112)

After Dinner: Chamomile tea or caffeine-free mint tea

FAQ

1. **Why Healthy Indulgence? How is this plan different from other well-known diets and nutrition plans?**

If you look at most other plans on the market today, you'll find that they encourage you to follow their philosophies for a limited period of time. Be it 14 days or 28 days, that's all well and good for people who want to temporarily lose weight for an upcoming event. But what happens after the 28 days? Well, most people go back to their old way of life, and any weight-loss that has occurred comes right back.

The Healthy Indulgence plan is not a temporary diet and doesn't prescribe a set regimen for a short period of time. This plan is a way of life, and it has been created to not only change the way you think about food, but to also give you practical tools to implement a long-term lifestyle change.

2. **Sima, you want me to eat more?! How is that going to help me lose weight?**

The key is not just to eat more—it's to eat more of the right things at the right time. Eating certain foods at certain times in the day and in the right combinations helps to keep your blood sugar stabilized, and helps your body function better, which in turn leads to weight-loss.

3. **How on earth can meditation help me lose weight? And I hate working out! Do I have to do it?**

When you wake up in the morning, your mind is booting up like a computer. It's ready to take on a brand-new day and your brain is the most receptive to new impressions at this time in the day. So if the first thing you do every morning is feed your social media addiction by logging on to your social profiles and reading about war and disaster, your mind will be infused with negative energy all day. Meditation helps you to cut through the chatter in your mind and gives you clarity so you are able to make wiser decisions and stay on track with your goals.

Meditation also helps keep you in top shape mentally, physically, and spiritually. As for the working out part of this question—I hope you're not serious. You should know by now that working out is an integral component of a healthy lifestyle. You don't have to endure a high-intensity workout every day to be in shape. The Healthy Indulgence specialized workout routine can be done anywhere and it takes less time than you think. The workout only requires two dumbbells and a yoga mat, and is individually targeted to your needs.

4. Your program includes carbs in every meal? But carbs are the enemy!
Carbs are not the enemy, and there's no way to get that athletic body you want without eating carbs. Carbs are necessary for your body and can be broken down into simple carbs and complex carbs. Simple carbs can provide your body with quick bursts of energy (think orange juice) while complex carbs will provide your body with long-lasting energy (think yam or sweet potato). You need carbs to function.

5. I hate cooking. Why do I need to cook my own food?
It's funny you say that. I'm not crazy about cooking either. I have plenty of other things to do. Which is why each and every recipe in this plan takes approximately 30 minutes to cook and prepare. It's cheaper than eating out and you know exactly what goes into it. The recipes in this book are nothing fancy; simplicity is one of the key things to learn if you want to get into the best shape of your life.

6. Can I still have bread, chocolate, and wine?
Absolutely. Eat (or drink) it and enjoy it, too. My only request is that you don't feel guilty about it. A big part of my plan is no deprivation. If you want to eat cake, that's perfectly fine with me. The key is to not eat it every day, and to eliminate food guilt. Enjoying what you eat in moderation is a better path to a healthy life than starving yourself. Plus, if I tell you that you can never have bread, chocolate, and wine, all your mind will want to do is have bread, chocolate, and wine. We are human. We want what we can't have and the more we can't have it, the more we want it and the more we'll find ways to get it. However, if you insist on eating these foods every day, it will negate all the benefits of a diet based on a proper PCF combo.

7. Is your plan safe for pregnant women and kids?
Yes it is, for the most part. There are few exceptions such as bee pollen and maca powder which are not recommended for pregnant or breastfeeding women or children. Nevertheless, as always you need to consult with your physician before starting any new diet plan.

8. What if I'm not a snacker or if I skip meals?

You will still lose weight if you follow this plan for the meals you do eat. A word to the wise: It's okay to skip snacks, but don't skip breakfast, lunch, or dinner. Breakfast in particular is the most important meal of the day. You need to eat a healthy PCF combo to start your day. It's important to eat every three hours to keep your blood sugar stable because when your blood sugar is out of whack, the first thing you're going to crave is sugar or junk food and the last thing you're going to crave is a PCF-approved meal. Keeping your blood sugar stable will curb junk food cravings, which will help keep you on track.

Connect with Sima

Nothing makes me happier than knowing I was able to make a difference in someone's life, so I would love it if you shared your success stories with me. I want to hear from you! Email me, follow me on Instagram, tweet me, or leave a comment—I will read them all. Upload your photos to Instagram and use the hashtag #simacohen, #healthy-indulgence, #simashealthyindulgence, #pcfcombo, #pcfdiet, or #abundantliving so we can show the world what living in indulgence is all about!

Website: www.simacohen.com
Facebook: simacohenofficial
Instagram: @simacohenofficial
Twitter: @simaofficial
Youtube: Sima Cohen Official
Email: sima@simacohen.com

Resources

I am delighted to introduce you to the following companies with whom I have had the utmost pleasure of working and collaborating. I highly respect their values and dedication of the management and staff to their consumers. I believe these companies are more like partners as their philosophy and goals are perfectly aligned with mine. These partner companies and I all have the same vision of creating and maintaining a healthy lifestyle and I am proud to introduce them to you.

- FRÉ Skincare
  FRÉ is the first luxury skincare range for women who work out, specially formulated for sweating skin. With its breakthrough natural formula Argania Active Complex©, made of organic Argan oil, stem cells and water-extract of the leaf, FRÉ skincare set is a comprehensive 3-step facial skincare treatment that creates healthy, fresh, and resilient skin for active women. FRÉ ultra-light and fresh formulas prevent sweat-induced skin damage from breakouts to dryness and premature aging and promote a natural glow. For every set sold, an Argan Tree of Life is planted to empower women communities who harvest Argan oil in Morocco, and protect our planet.

  www.freskincare.com
  Instagram: @freskincare
  Facebook: https://www.facebook.com/freskincare
  Twitter: https://twitter.com/freskincare

- Health and Wealth Lovers
  Shadi Pazeshki and Health And Wealth Lovers offers kangen water for life. Consuming Kangen Water especially before, during, and after my workouts has made a big difference in my hydration efficiency and overall performance. It can be used for many purposes including drinking, cooking, and skincare. They understand that the basis of vitality and long life is water and want to bring Kangen water into your home.

  www.alkalinehealsyou.com
  Instagram: @healthandwealthlovers
  Twitter: @healthandwealthlovers
  Facebook.com/healthandwealthlovers
  YouTube: Youtube.com/healthandwealthlovers

- Melissa's
With an amazing online shopping experience and exceptional delivery service, Melissa's is my #1 choice for produce. Within the Melissa's/World Variety Produce, Inc. warehouse, you can find the freshest fruits, vegetables, specialty foods, and packaged items—quality products with exceptional value and first-class service. Melissa's is currently the largest distributor of specialty produce in the United States.

  www.melissas.com
  Facebook.com/melissasproduce
  Instagram: @melissasproduce
  Twitter: @melissasproduce
  YouTube: Youtube.com/melissasworldvariety

- Panorama Meats/Western Grassfed Beef
Panorama Meats works with family ranchers throughout the U.S. to provide 100% grass fed and grass finished beef from cattle that were NEVER treated with added hormones or antibiotics—ever. Panorama Organic Grass-Fed Beef is Certified Organic and can be found at Whole Foods Markets. Western Grassfed Beef can be found online at www.westerngrassfedbeef.com, on Amazon, and in select retailers.

  www.panoramameats.com
  Facebook: https://www.facebook.com/panoramameats/
  Instagram: @panoramameats
  Twitter: @PanoramaMeats
  Pinterest: https://www.pinterest.com/panoramameats

  www.westerngrassfedbeef.com
  Facebook: https://www.facebook.com/WesternGrassFedBeef
  Instagram: @westerngrassfed
  Twitter: @WesternGrassfed
  Pinterest: https://www.pinterest.com/westerngrassfedbeef

- reCAP Mason Jars
Transform your mason jars with reCAP mason jar lids and accessories. Invented by engineer and problem-solving mom, Karen Rzepecki, reCAP allows you to use your mason jars in fun and creative ways. Versatile and multi-functional, reCAP is the must-have kitchen companion for storing, pouring, and serving any variety of mason jar creations.

  Facebook: https://www.facebook.com/reCAPMasonJars/
  Instagram: @recapmasonjars

- Sadaf
Sadaf Foods is a leading manufacturer and distributor of Mediterranean and specialty foods. Sadaf products are available in all ethnic supermarkets. They offer a variety of products ready to consume like sauces, stews, and traditional Mediterranean cuisine. I love their variety of unique items such as black garlic, rose water, and saffron, which added an incredible flavor to my recipes.

  www.sadaf.com
  Instagram: @sadaf_foods

- Wellness to Be
Bita Yadidi, doctor of Acupuncture and Eastern Medicine, is founder of Wellness to Be, in Beverly Hills, a center for women focusing on restoring and rejuvenating the mind, body, and spirit. Bita is my guru when it comes to medicine and acupuncture. The center provides health care and services emphasizing a holistic approach treating customers through acupuncture, herbal medicine, lifestyle coaching, and movement arts.

  www.WellnessToBe.com
  Bita@WellnessToBe.com
  Instagram: @wellnesstobe

Additional Resources

It is my pleasure to offer the following companies as my resource list. These are the companies that I go to and trust to provide the ingredients, products, and services that are aligned with my brand and promote healthy living. They have also supplied me with advice and support about their products and other alternatives.

Active Apparel & Equipment
- Lorna Jane
  www.lornajane.com
- Athleta
  www.athleta.com
- Style Runner
  www.stylerunner.com
- Pampelone Clothing
  pampelone.com
- BI Sportswear
  bisportswear.com
- Onzie
  onzie.com
- Fabletics
  fabletics.com

Appliances
- Kitchen Aid
  www.kitchenaid.com
- Omega
  http://omegaappliances.com
- Excalibur
  www.appliancesconnection.com
- Ninja
  www.ninjakitchen.com
- KitchenIQ
  www.kitcheniq.com

Bars
- Epic Bar
  www.epicbar.com
- Exo Protein
  www.exoprotein.com
- GoMacro
  www.gomacro.com
- Health Warrior
  www.healthwarrior.com
- Kind
  www.kindsnacks.com
- Lara
  www.larabar.com
- Mad Macro
  www.madmacro.com
- Primal Kitchen
  www.primalkitchen.com
- Pure
  www.pureorganic.com
- RXBar
  www.rxbar.com
- Shanti
  www.shanti.bar

Beauty
- Pacific Beauty
  www.pacificabeauty.com"www.pacificabeauty.com

- Life Elements
  www.lifeelements.com
- Pearl Butter
  www.pearlbutter.com
- FabFitFun
  www.fabfitfun.com
- Acure Organics
  www.acureorganics.com
- Yes To
  www.yesto.com
- Fre
  www.freskincare.com

Beverages
- Bai Water
  www.drinkbai.com
- Choffy
  www.choffy.com
- Crio Bru
  www.criobru.com
- Drink Live
  www.drinklive.com
- Harmless Harvest
  www.harmlessharvest.com
- Health And Wealth Lovers
  www.healthandwealth.com
- LaCroix Water
  lacroixwater.com
- Life Wtr
  www.lifewtr.com

Breads
- Le Pain Quotidien
  www.lepainquotidien.com
- Milk & Eggs
  www.milkandeggs.com
- Bread Los Angeles
  www.breadlosangeles.com

- Bread Lounge
  www.breadlounge.com

Broth
- Osso Good Bone Broth
  www.ossogoodbones.com
- Pacific Foods
  www.pacificfoods.com
- Western Grassfed Beef
  www.westerngrassfedbeef.com

Books
- *Marianne Williamson's Return to Love*
- *From Tears to Triumph* by Marianne Williamson
- *Illuminata* by Marianne Williamson
- *The Law of Divine Compensation: On Work, Money and Miracles* by Marianne Williamson
- *A Course in Miracles* by The Foundation For Inner Peace
- *The Four Agreements: A Practical Guide to Personal* Freedom by Don Miguel Ruiz
- *The Monk Who Sold His Ferrari* by Robin Sharma
- *The Perfect Blend* by Tess Masters
- *Barefoot Contessa Fool Proof* by Ina Garten
- *Make It Ahead* by Ina Garten
- *Giada's Feel Good Food* by Giada De Laurentis

Catering
- Two Peas Inc.
  www.twopeasinc.com

- Le Pain Quotidien
  www.lepainquotidien.com

Chocolate
- Cocoa Parlor
  www.cocoaparlor.com
- Lindt chocolate
  www.Lindtchocolate.com
- Raaka Chocolate
  www.raakachocolate.com
- Askinoisie Chocolate
  www.askinosie.com
- Mast Brothers
  www.mastbrothers.com
- Map Chocolate
  www.mapchocolate.com

Coffee & Tea
- Bulletproof
  www.bulletproof.com
- Chameleon Cold Brew
  www.chameleoncoldbrew.com
- Klio Tea
  www.kliotea.com
- Yogi Tea
  www.yogiproducts.com
- Teaonic
  www.teaonic.com
- Big Heart Tea
  www.bighearttea.com
- Stumptown Coffee
  www.stumptowncoffee.com

Cookies and Crackers
- Enjoy Life
  www.enjoylifefoods.com
- Mary's gone crackers
  www.marysgonecrackers.com

Dairy-free Milks, Yogurts, and Cheeses
- New Barn unsweetened almond milk
  www.thenewbarn.com
- Pacific Foods
  www.pacificfoods.com
- Pop and Bottle
  www.popandbottle.com
- The Coconut Cult
  www.thecoconutcult.com
- Greek Gods Yogurt
  www.greekgodsyogurt.com
- Milk & Eggs
  www.milkandeggs.com

Dressings & Sauces
- Bragg
  www.bragg.com
- Eden Foods
  www.edenfoods.com
- Horsetooth Hot Sauce
  www.horsetoothhotsauce.com
- Primal Kitchen
  www.primalkitchen.com
- Rao's
  www.raos.com
- Newman's Own
  www.newmansown.com
- Saucy Lips
  www.sauclipsfoods.com
- Tessmae's All Natural
  www.tessmaes.com
- Tuttorosso Tomatoes
  www.tuttorossotomatoes.com

Eco-Friendly Cleaning Supplies
- Bio Kleen Home
  www.biokleenhome.com

- Mrs. Meyers Clean Day
  www.mrsmeyers.com
- Casa bella clean
  www.casabella.com

Elixirs & Juices
- Harmless Harvest
  www.harmlessharvest.com
- Juice Crafters
  www.juicecrafters.com
- Juice Served Here
  www.juiceservedhere.com
- Moon Juice
  www.moonjuiceshop.com
- Pressed Juicery
  www.pressedjuicery.com
- Temple Turmeric
  templeturmeric.com
- Juicero
  www.juicero.com
- Suja Juices
  www.sujajuice.com
- Temple Turmeric
  www.templeturmeric.com
- Daily Harvest
  www.daily-harvest.com

Eggs
- Milk & Eggs
  www.milkandeggs.com
- Chino Valley Ranchers
  www.chinovalleyranchers.com
- Golden Fresh Eggs
  www.goldenfresheggs.com
- Organic Valley Eggs
  www.organicvalleyeggs.coop
- Vital Farms
  www.vitalfarms.com

Fish
- Loki Fish Company
  www.lokifish.com
- Sizzlefish
  www.sizzlefish.com

Meat & Poultry
- Panorama Meats
  www.panoramameats.com
  www.westerngrassfedbeef.com
- Western Grassfed Beef
  www.westerngrassfedbeef.com
- Applegate
  www.applegate.com
- Maple Leaf Farms
  www.mapleleaffarms.com
- Petaluma Poultry
  www.petalumapoultry.com

Flours & Grains
- Bob's Red Mill
  www.bobsredmill.com
- Ancient Harvest
  www.ancientharvest.com
- Arrowhead Mills
  www.arrowheadmills.com

Granola & Oats
- Purely Elizabeth
  www.purelyelizabeth.com
- Kessons Kitchen
  www.kessonskitchen.com

Herbs, Spices, & Seasoning
- Frontier Co-op Natural Products
  www.frontiercoop.com
- Bragg
  www.bragg.com

- Paleo Powder
  www.paleopowderseasoning.com
- Primal Palate
  www.primalpalate.com
- Sadaf
  www.sadaf.com
- Spice Cave Organic Spice Blends
  www.thespicecave.com
- Spice Hound
  www.spicehound.com
- Temple Turmeric
  www.templeturmeric.com
- Pereg Gourmet
  www.pereg-gourmet.com
- Pranayums
  www.pranayums.com

Juicers
- Omega Juicers
  www.omegajuicers.com

Kitchenware
- KitchenIQ
  www.kitcheniq.com
- Kitchen Aid
  www.kitchenaid.com
- reCAP Mason Jars
  www.recapmasonjars.com
- Eco Jarz
  www.ecojarz.com
- Global
  www.global-knife.com
- Pottery Barn
  www.potterybarn.com
- Williams Sonoma
  http://www.williams-sonoma.com/

Magazines/Publications
- *DailyOM*
  http://dailyom.com
- *MindBodyGreen*
  www.mindbodygreen.com
- *O, the Oprah Magazine*
  http://www.oprah.com/app/o-magazine.html
- *Rachel Ray Everyday*
  www.rachaelraymag.com
- *Martha Stewart Living*
  www.marthastewart.com
- *Cooking Light*
  www.cookinglight.com
- *LA Mom Magazine*
  www.lamommagazine.com
- *Oloxir*
  www.oloxir.com
- Face the Current
  www.facethecurrent.com

Nut & Seed Butters
- Artisana Organics
  www.premierorganics.org
- Cracked Nut Butter
  www.crackednutbutter.com
- Justin's
  www.justins.com
- Living Nutz
  www.livingnutz.com
- MeeNut Butter
  www.meeeatpaleo.com
- Nuts
  www.nuts.com
- Sun Butter
  www.sunbutter.com
- Wilderness Poets
  www.wildernesspoets.com

- Living Intentions
  www.livingintentions.com
- Ag Standard
  www.enjoytheflavor.com
- Coldwater Canyon Provisions
  www.coldwaterprovisions.com
- Spread The Love
  www.spreadthelovefoods.com

Nuts & Seeds
- Sadaf
  www.sadaf.com
- Navitas Naturals
  www.navitasorganics.com/home
- Nutiva
  www.nutiva.com
- Melissa's
  www.melissas.com
- Berry Man Inc.
  www.theberryman.com/wordpress

Oils & Vinegars
- Bragg
  www.bragg.com
- Nutiva
  www.nutiva.com
- O Olive Oil and Vinegar
  www.ooliveoil.com
- Omega Nutrition
  www.omeganutrition.com
- Pasolivo
  www.pasolivo.com
- Spectrum Organics
  www.spectrumorganics.com
- Sadaf
  www.sadaf.com
- Sun Coast Gold
  www.suncoastgoldmac.com

Probiotics
- The Beauty Chef
  www.thebeautychef.com
- Temple Turmeric
  www.templeturmeric.com
- Vital Proteins
  www.vitalproteins.com
- GoodBelly Probiotics
  www.goodbelly.com
- Farmhouse Cultures
  www.daily-harvest.com

Produce
- Melissa's
  www.melissas.com
- Berry Man Inc.
  www.theberryman.com/wordpress
- Zuma Valley
  www.zumavalley.com

Protein Powders
- Philosophie
  www.thephilosophie.com
- Garden of Life
  www.gardenoflife.com/content
- Sun Warrior
  www.sunwarrior.com
- Vega
  www.myvega.com
- Vital Proteins
  www.vitalproteins.com
- Moon Juice
  www.moonjuiceshop.com

Sea Salt
- Jacobsen Salt
  www.jacobsensalt.com
- Celtic Sea Salt
  www.celticseasalt.com

Superfoods
- Navitas Naturals
  www.navitasorganics.com
- E3live
  www.e3live.com
- Philosophie
  www.thephilosophie.com
- Sun Potion
  www.sunpotion.com
- Essential Living Foods
  www.essentiallivingfoods.com

Supplements
- Trulix
  https://trulixnaturals.com
- Vital Proteins
  www.vitalproteins.com
- EBoost
- www.eboost.com
- Sun Potion
  www.sunpotion.com
- Organic Mushroom Nutrition
  www.ommushrooms.com
  Sweeteners

Sweeteners
- Coconut Secret
  www.coconutsecret.com
- Maple Valley AG
  www.maplevalleyag.com
- Navitas Naturals
  www.navitasorganics.com
- Nutiva
  www.nutiva.com
- Big Tree Organic
  www.bigtreeorganic.com
- Wedderspoon
  www.wedderspoon.com

Wine
- Del Dotto-Vineyards
  www.deldottovineyards.com
- Fit Vine
  www.fitvinewine.com

Index

sriracha, 78, 162, 177
strawberries, 61, 180, 220, 226
Strawberry Rose Oatmeal, 58
Stuffed Sweet Potatoes with Warm Bean
    Salad, 114
sumac, 70
sunflower seeds, 43, 62, 69, 70, 74, 83,
    89, 96, 107, 137, 144, 150
Super Bark, 214
superfoods, 7, 17-21
sweet potatoes, 95, 114, 163, 171
Swiss cheese, 86

Taco Salad On the Go, 111
tahini, 20, 44, 70, 73, 90, 109, 114, 119,
    153, 162, 168, 179
tarragon, 81, 161
tartine, 48
The Kabob To My Naan, 70
thyme, 73, 100, 141, 177
tomato, 44, 46, 65, 69, 70, 73, 76, 89, 90,
    99, 107, 109, 111, 114, 119, 125, 137,
    144, 186
tomato paste, 65, 137, 159
tuna, 104, 127, 134, 144, 167
Tuna, Lemme Upgrade Ya, 166
Turkey Bacon, 65, 90

turkey breast, 141
Turkey Tahini Sandwich, 90
turmeric, 22, 48, 52, 95, 100, 102, 119,
    120, 138, 141, 142, 149, 192, 194
Turmeric Latte, 194

vanilla extract, 50, 57, 62, 63, 149, 156,
    180, 213, 217, 218, 222, 225, 229
vegan butter, 141
vegan mayo, 81
vegetable broth, 95, 96, 99, 100

walnuts, 95, 106, 112, 127, 142, 153, 164,
    183, 184, 218, 229, 231
wasabi powder, 134
watermelon radishes, 69, 83
Weekday Earth Detox Soup, 96
wheat germ, 19, 48, 54, 84
Whole Wheat, 44, 48, 65, 67, 69, 70, 74,
    78, 81, 86, 89, 90, 95, 107, 159, 172,
    183

Your Kind of Granola Bars, 62

za'atar, 73
Zoodle My Noodle, 129
zucchini, 129

Conversion Charts
Metric and Imperial Conversions
(These conversions are rounded for convenience)

Ingredient	Cups/Tablespoons/Teaspoons	Ounces	Grams/Milliliters
Butter	1 cup/ 16 tablespoons/ 2 sticks	8 ounces	230 grams
Cheese, shredded	1 cup	4 ounces	110 grams
Cream cheese	1 tablespoon	0.5 ounce	14.5 grams
Cornstarch	1 tablespoon	0.3 ounce	8 grams
Flour, all-purpose	1 cup/1 tablespoon	4.5 ounces/0.3 ounce	125 grams/8 grams
Flour, whole wheat	1 cup	4 ounces	120 grams
Fruit, dried	1 cup	4 ounces	120 grams
Fruits or veggies, chopped	1 cup	5 to 7 ounces	145 to 200 grams
Fruits or veggies, puréed	1 cup	8.5 ounces	245 grams
Honey, maple syrup, or corn syrup	1 tablespoon	.75 ounce	20 grams
Liquids: cream, milk, water, or juice	1 cup	8 fluid ounces	240 milliliters
Oats	1 cup	5.5 ounces	150 grams
Salt	1 teaspoon	0.2 ounces	6 grams
Spices: cinnamon, cloves, ginger, or nutmeg (ground)	1 teaspoon	0.2 ounce	5 milliliters
Sugar, brown, firmly packed	1 cup	7 ounces	200 grams
Sugar, white	1 cup/1 tablespoon	7 ounces/0.5 ounce	200 grams/12.5 grams
Vanilla extract	1 teaspoon	0.2 ounce	4 grams

Oven Temperatures

Fahrenheit	Celsius	Gas Mark
225°	110°	¼
250°	120°	½
275°	140°	1
300°	150°	2
325°	160°	3
350°	180°	4
375°	190°	5
400°	200°	6
425°	220°	7
450°	230°	8

Liquids

8 fluid ounces = 1 cup = ½ pint
16 fluid ounces = 2 cups = 1 pint
32 fluid ounces = 4 cups = 1 quart
128 fluid ounces = 16 cups = 1 gallon

Skyhorse Publishing books may be purchased in bulk at special discounts for sales promotion, corporate gifts, fund-raising, or educational purposes. Special editions can also be created to specifications. For details, contact the Special Sales Department, Skyhorse Publishing, 307 West 36th Street, 11th Floor, New York, NY 10018 or info@skyhorsepublishing.com.

Skyhorse® and Skyhorse Publishing® are registered trademarks of Skyhorse Publishing, Inc.®, a Delaware corporation.

Visit our website at www.skyhorsepublishing.com.

10 9 8 7 6 5 4 3 2 1

Library of Congress Cataloging-in-Publication Data is available on file.

Cover design by Jane Sheppard
Cover photograph by Delaram Pourabdi

Print ISBN: 978-1-5107-2807-3
Ebook ISBN: 978-1-5107-2808-0

Printed in China

Disclaimer:
All the material contained in this book is meant for informational and educational purposes only, and the book's use is solely at your own risk. The information contained in this book is based on author's personal and professional experience and research, and is not a substitute for professional and medical diagnosis or treatment. Consult with a physician or your healthcare professional concerning questions about your health, nutrition, and medical-related needs. All readers who have any kind of medical condition, or are taking any form of prescription medication, or have food allergies, should consult with their physicians before making any changes to their current diets. The publisher and author are not responsible for any harmful effects or adverse consequences arising from the use of the methods, recipes, products, and information contained in this book.

SIMA